1969

This book may be kept

FOURTEEN DAYS

N

THE REFERENCE SHELF   VOLUME 41 NUMBER 4

REPRESENTATIVE AMERICAN SPEECHES: 1968-1969

EDITED BY LESTER THONSSEN

Professor of Speech
Metropolitan State College of Colorado at Denver

THE H. W. WILSON COMPANY
NEW YORK   1969

THE REFERENCE SHELF

The books in this series contain reprints of articles, excerpts from books, and addresses on current issues and social trends in the United States and other countries. There are six separately bound numbers in each volume, all of which are generally published in the same calendar year. One number is a collection of recent speeches; each of the others is devoted to a single subject and gives background information and discussion from various points of view, concluding with a comprehensive bibliography.

Subscribers to the current volume receive the books as issued. The subscription rate is $14 in the United States and Canada ($17 foreign) for a volume of six numbers. Single numbers are $3.50 each in the United States and Canada ($4 foreign).

PREFACE

Writing in *The Christian Science Monitor*, William H. Stringer reflected on an element which was missing and sorely missed in 1968: "any kind of eloquent public utterance, or anything much in the way of inspired statement." "A nation—a world—" he continued, "can benefit when someone lifts up its hopes. This year there was a rhetoric gap." In 1968, Americans lost through assassination their "natural-born great speaker" Dr. Martin Luther King, Jr., and "many of President Johnson's homilies were not much calculated to rouse the citizens." Mr. Stringer surmised that the oratory of threat, while flowing in to fill the vacuum, "failed to appeal to the basic morality of America."

While some critics would doubtless debate the Stringer thesis, I suspect a general feeling prevailed that the year did not produce an abundance of good political oratory. Surely the speechmaking during the campaign did not rise to superlative heights. And elsewhere there was an apparent reluctance to speak out eloquently—if not a fear of speaking out—on the most volatile topics.

Reflecting on these circumstances, I recalled a passage in his "Eulogy on Webster" in which Rufus Choate spoke of two kinds of oratory—the one expressing a national consciousness of despair and decline; the other, the buoyant spirit of national ascent. A substantial part of American oratory in 1968 and early 1969 came unfortunately close to falling in the first category. Perhaps there is a moral in Choate's analysis:

> In looking over the public remains of . . . [Webster's] oratory [he wrote], it is striking to remark how, even in that most sober and massive understanding and nature, you see gathered and expressed the characteristic sentiments and the passing time of our America. It is the strong old oak which ascends before you; yet our soil, our heaven, are attested in it as perfectly as if it were a flower

3

that could grow in no other climate and in no other hour of the year or day. Let me instance in one thing only. It is a peculiarity of some schools of eloquence that they embody and utter, not merely the individual genius and character of the speaker, but a national consciousness—a national era, a mood, a hope, a dread, a despair—in which you listen to the spoken history of the time. There is an eloquence of an expiring nation, such as seems to sadden the glorious speech of Demosthenes; such as breathes grand and gloomy from the visions of the prophets of the last days of Israel and Judah; such as gave a spell to the expression of Grattan and of Kossuth—the sweetest, most mournful, most awful of the words which man may utter, or which man may hear—the eloquence of a perishing nation. There is another eloquence, in which the national consciousness of a young or renewed and vast strength, of trust in a dazzling, certain, and limitless future, an inward glorying in victories yet to be won, sounds out as by voice of clarion, challenging to contest for the highest prize of earth; such as that in which the leader of Israel in its first days holds up to the new nation the Land of Promise; such as that which in the well-imagined speeches scattered by Livy over the history of the "majestic series of victories" speaks the Roman consciousness of growing aggrandizement which should subject the world; such as that through which, at the tribunes of her revolution, in the bulletins of her rising soldier, France told to the world her dream of glory. And of this kind somewhat is ours; cheerful, hopeful, trusting, as befits youth and spring; the eloquence of a State beginning to ascend to the first class of power, eminence, and consideration, and conscious of itself. It is to no purpose that they tell you it is in bad taste; that it partakes of arrogance and vanity; that a true national good breeding would not know, or seem to know, whether the nation is old or young; whether the tides of being are in their flow or ebb; whether these coursers of the sun are sinking slowly to rest, wearied with a journey of a thousand years, or just bounding from the Orient unbreathed. Higher laws than those of taste determine the consciousness of nations. Higher laws than those of taste determine the general forms of the expression of that consciousness. Let the downward age of America find its orators and poets and artists to erect its spirit, or grace and soothe its dying; be it ours to go up with Webster to the Rock, the Monument, the Capitol, and bid "the distant generations hail!"

In this thirty-second volume of the series, I include a selected group of fifteen addresses. Whether or not they are "great" or even "representative" must be settled by each reader. Since I do not much like either term, I should rather make them meet a simple, personal test: Are they worthy of remembrance? In my judgment, they are.

For favoring me with valuable counsel and assistance, I express my gratitude to John Jamieson and Beth Freedman of The H. W. Wilson Company, Dean Keats R. McKinney of the Metropolitan State College, Margaret Robb of the University of Colorado, Ota Thomas Reynolds of Hunter College, Elizabeth F. Russell, C. W. Reynolds, Ruth Taylor, Marva McKinney, Dorothea Thonssen, Sandi Schloffman, and Dr. Ward Darley and Dr. E. Stewart Taylor of the University of Colorado Medical School in Denver.

LESTER THONSSEN

Denver, Colorado
August 1969

CONTENTS

PREFACE   3

A QUESTION OF SURVIVAL

Richard M. Nixon. The Antiballistic Missile System . . .   9

Jerome B. Wiesner. An Argument Against the ABM . .   19

REFLECTIONS ON WAR, PROTEST, AND THE GOVERNANCE OF MAN

George Wald. A Generation in Search of a Future   33

John Hope Franklin. Martin Luther King and American Traditions   45

Malcolm Moos. Darkness Over the Ivory Tower   55

Shirley Chisholm. It Is Time to Reassess Our National Priorities   68

INTERNATIONAL PERSPECTIVES

Edward M. Kennedy. China Policy for the Seventies . . .   73

Walter B. Wriston. A Long View of the Short Run   89

Mike Mansfield. A Pacific Perspective   98

Postscripts to Electoral Choice

Richard M. Nixon. Inaugural Address 113

Harold F. Harding. A Matter of Doubt and Grave
    Concern 121

Views on the Struggles for Equality

Armando M. Rodriguez. This Is Our Quest: To Fight
    for the Right 129

Separatism or Integration: Which Way for America? ... 143

    Robert S. Browne. A Case for Separation 144

    Bayard Rustin. Toward Integration as a Goal 156

The Long Journey Home

Charlotte T. Reid. A Tribute to Dwight D. Eisenhower 165

Appendix: Biographical Notes 169

Cumulative Author Index: 1960-1961—1968-1969 174

A QUESTION OF SURVIVAL

THE ANTIBALLISTIC MISSILE SYSTEM [1]

RICHARD M. NIXON [2]

In his farewell address to the American people on January 17, 1961, President Dwight D. Eisenhower warned of the grave implications of the "conjunction of an immense military establishment and a large arms industry." "In the councils of government," he remarked, "we must guard against the acquisition of unwarranted influence, whether sought or unsought, by the military-industrial complex." This reminder is even more awesomely pertinent today than when it was uttered. For arms races have scarcely slackened and expenditures for war equipment have soared to frightening heights.

An uneasy relationship continues between the two powers which possess massive nuclear strength. And the strategy of both depends importantly on what is often called the second-strike capability. This is the capacity for retaliatory action, which presumably will serve as a deterrent to offensive strikes. Clearly, such strategy presupposes a rough balance of strength, rather than a nuclear superiority so great that a retaliatory strike would be impossible.

Currently at the center of this disturbing problem is the proposal to establish and deploy the antiballistic missile defense system. The question is not new. Billions of dollars have already been spent on missile defense research over the past decade. In late 1967, Robert S. McNamara, then Secretary of Defense in the Johnson administration, came out for a limited system—the Sentinel plan—which received congressional approval. It called for the construction of fifteen or more antimissile sites, chiefly near large population centers—a circumstance which immediately provoked sharp objections from its many critics. The new decision by President Nixon changed the basic deployment plan.

At his televised news conference in the White House on March 14, 1969, President Nixon made his first major decision

[1] Advance text of the President's announcement and transcript of his statement at his news conference, the White House, Washington, D.C., March 14, 1969. Text furnished by the Office of the Press Secretary to the President.

[2] For biographical note, see Appendix.

9

since taking office. Following several weeks of consultations with his advisers, and in the midst of deep public concern over his announcement, he came out for a modified plan—a "safeguard" system—which eventually would consist of twelve sites near the nation's retaliatory defense establishments. The estimated cost would be about $7 billion.

Reprinted below are two statements: the first is a text of the announcement as released to the press by the Office of the White House press secretary prior to the news conference; the second, the actual text of the President's remarks at the opening of the conference. Except for three minor changes, the speech text conforms to the transcript which was recorded and published by the New York *Times* on March 15. Students of public address may be interested in examining the way in which a printed release was converted to an extemporaneous statement before the newsmen and television audience. The audience, incidentally, was large. Administration aides estimated that some 43 per cent of the nation's television sets were tuned in when the President made his opening statement.

Advance Text of Statement

Immediately after assuming office, I requested the Secretary of Defense to review the program initiated by the last administration to deploy the Sentinel ballistic missile defense system.

The Department of Defense presented a full statement of the alternatives at the last two meetings of the National Security Council. These alternatives were reviewed there in the light of the security requirements of the United States and of their probable impact on East-West relations, with particular reference to the prospects for strategic arms negotiations.

After carefully considering the alternatives, I have reached the following conclusions: (1) the concept on which the Sentinel program of the previous administration was based should be substantially modified; (2) the safety of our country requires that we should proceed now with the development and construction of the new system in a carefully phased program; (3) this program will be reviewed annually from the point of view of (a) technical developments,

(b) the threat, (c) the diplomatic context, including any talks on arms limitation.

The modified system has been designed so that its defensive intent is unmistakable. It will be implemented not according to some fixed, theoretical schedule but in a manner clearly related to our periodic analysis of the threat. The first deployment covers two missile sites; the first of these will not be completed before 1973. Any further delay would set this date back by at least two additional years. The program for fiscal year 1970 is the minimum necessary to maintain the security of our nation.

This measured deployment is designed to fulfill three objectives:

1. Protection of our land-based retaliatory forces against a direct attack by the Soviet Union;

2. Defense of the American people against the kind of nuclear attack which Communist China is likely to be able to mount within the decade;

3. Protection against the possibility of accidental attacks from any source.

In the review leading up to this decision, we considered three possible options in addition to this program: A deployment which would attempt to defend U.S. cities against an attack by the Soviet Union; a continuation of the Sentinel program approved by the previous administration; an indefinite postponement of deployment while continuing research and development.

I rejected these options for the following reasons:

Although every instinct motivates me to provide the American people with complete protection against a major nuclear attack, it is not now within our power to do so. The heaviest defense system we considered, one designed to protect our major cities, still could not prevent a catastrophic level of U.S. fatalities from a deliberate all-out Soviet attack. And it might look to an opponent like the prelude to an offensive strategy threatening the Soviet deterrent.

The Sentinel system approved by the previous administration provided more capabilities for the defense of cities than the program I am recommending, but it did not provide protection against some threats to our retaliatory forces which have developed subsequently. Also, the Sentinel system had the disadvantage that it could be misinterpreted as the first step toward the construction of a heavy system.

Giving up all construction of missile defense poses too many risks. Research and Development does not supply the answer to many technical issues that only operational experience can provide. The Soviet Union has engaged in a buildup of its strategic forces larger than was envisaged in 1967, when the decision to deploy Sentinel was made. The following is illustrative of recent Soviet activity:

1. The Soviets have already deployed an ABM [antiballistic missile] system which protects to some degree a wide area centered around Moscow. We will not have a comparable capability for over four years. We believe the Soviet Union is continuing their ABM development, directed either toward improving this initial system or, more likely, making substantially better second-generation ABM components.

2. The Soviet Union is continuing the deployment of very large missiles with warheads capable of destroying our hardened Minuteman forces.

3. The Soviet Union has also been substantially increasing the size of their submarine-launched ballistic missile force.

4. The Soviets appear to be developing a semiorbital nuclear weapon system.

In addition to these developments, the Chinese threat against our population, as well as the danger of an accidental attack, cannot be ignored. By approving this system, it is possible to reduce U.S. fatalities to a minimal level in the event of a Chinese nuclear attack in the 1970's, or in an accidental attack from any source. No President with the responsibility for the lives and security of the American people could fail to provide this protection.

The gravest responsibility which I bear as President of the United States is for the security of the nation. Our nuclear forces defend not only ourselves but our allies as well. The imperative that our nuclear deterrent remain secure beyond any possible doubt requires that the United States must take steps now to insure that our strategic retaliatory forces will not become vulnerable to a Soviet attack.

Modern technology provides several choices in seeking to insure the survival of our retaliatory forces.

First, we could increase the number of sea- and land-based missiles and bombers. I have ruled out this course because it provides only marginal improvement of our deterrent, while it could be misinterpreted by the Soviets as an attempt to threaten their deterrent. It would therefore stimulate an arms race.

A second option is to harden further our ballistic missile forces by putting them in more strongly reinforced underground silos. But our studies show that hardening by itself is not adequate protection against foreseeable advances in the accuracy of Soviet offensive forces.

The third option was to begin a measured construction on an active defense of our retaliatory forces.

I have chosen the third option.

The system will use components previously developed for the Sentinel system. However, the deployment will be changed to reflect the new concept. We will provide for local defense of selected Minuteman missile sites and an area defense designed to protect our bomber bases and our command and control authorities. In addition, this new system will provide a defense of the continental United States against an accidental attack and will provide substantial protection against the kind of attack which the Chinese Communists may be capable of launching throughout the 1970's. This deployment will not require us to place missile and radar sites close to our major cities.

The present estimate is that the total cost of installing this system will be $6-$7 billion. However, because of the deliberate pace of the deployment, budgetary requests for the coming year can be substantially less—by about one half —than those asked for by the previous administration for the Sentinel system.

In making this decision, I have been mindful of my pledge to make every effort to move from an era of confrontation to an era of negotiation. The program I am recommending is based on a careful assessment of the developing Soviet and Chinese threats. I have directed the President's Foreign Intelligence Advisory Board—a nonpartisan group of distinguished private citizens—to make a yearly assessment of the threat, which will supplement our regular intelligence assessment. Each phase of the deployment will be reviewed to insure that we are doing as much as necessary but no more than that required by the threat existing at that time. Moreover, we will take maximum advantage of the information gathered from the initial deployment in designing the later phases of the program.

Since our deployment is to be closely related to the threat, it is subject to modification as the threat changes, either through negotiations or through unilateral actions by the Soviet Union or Communist China.

The program is not provocative. The Soviet retaliatory capability is not affected by our decision. The capability for surprise attack against our strategic forces is reduced. In other words, our program provides an incentive for a responsible Soviet weapons policy and for the avoidance of spiraling U.S. and Soviet strategic arms budgets.

I have taken cognizance of the view that beginning construction of a U.S. ballistic missile defense would complicate an agreement on strategic arms with the Soviet Union.

I do not believe that the evidence of the recent past bears out this contention. The Soviet interest in strategic talks was not deterred by the decision of the previous administration to deploy the Sentinel ABM system—in fact, it was formally announced shortly afterward. I believe that the modifications we have made in the previous program will give the Soviet Union even less reason to view our defense effort as an obstacle to talks. Moreover, I wish to emphasize that in any arms limitation talks with the Soviet Union, the United States will be fully prepared to discuss limitations on defensive as well as offensive weapons systems.

The question of ABM involves a complex combination of many factors:

—numerous, highly technical, often conflicting judgments;

—the costs;

—the relationship to prospects for reaching an agreement on limiting nuclear arms;

—the moral implications the deployment of a ballistic missile defense system has for many Americans;

—the impact of the decision on the security of the United States in this perilous age of nuclear arms.

I have weighed all these factors. I am deeply sympathetic to the concerns of private citizens and members of Congress that we do only that which is necessary for national security. This is why I am recommending a minimum program essential for our security. It is my duty as President to make certain that we do no less.

Opening Statement Delivered at News Conference

Ladies and gentlemen, today I am announcing a decision which I believe is vital for the security and defense of the United States, and also in the interest of peace throughout the world.

Last year a program, the Sentinel antiballistic missile program, was adopted. That program, as all listeners on television and radio and readers of newspapers know, has been the subject of very strong debate and controversy over the past few months.

After long study of all of the options available, I have concluded that the Sentinel program previously adopted should be substantially modified. The new program that I have recommended this morning to the leaders, and that I announce today, is one that perhaps best can be described as a safeguard program.

It is a safeguard against any attack by the Chinese Communists that we can foresee over the next ten years.

It is a safeguard of our deterrent system, which is increasingly vulnerable due to the advances that have been made by the Soviet Union since the year 1967, when the Sentinel program was first laid out.

It is a safeguard also against any irrational or accidental attack that might occur of less than massive magnitude which might be launched from the Soviet Union.

The program also does *not* do some things, which should be clearly understood. It does not provide defense for our cities, and for that reason the sites have been moved away from our major cities. I have made the decision with regard to this particular point because I found that there is no way, even if we were to expand the limited Sentinel system which was planned for some of our cities to a so-called heavy, or thick, system—there is no way that we can adequately defend our cities, without an unacceptable loss of life.

The only way that I have concluded that we can save lives—which is the primary purpose of our defense system—is to prevent war; and that is why the emphasis of this system is on protecting our deterrent, which is the best preventive for war.

The system differs from the previous Sentinel system in another major respect. The Sentinel system called for a fixed deployment schedule.

I believe that because of a number of reasons we should have a phase system. That is why, on an annual basis, the new safeguard system will be reviewed, and the review may bring about changes in the system based on our evaluation of three major points:

First, what our intelligence shows us with regard to the magnitude of the threat, whether from the Soviet Union or from the Chinese; and

Second, in terms of what our evaluation is of any talks that we are having by that time, or may be having, with regard to arms control; and

Finally, because we believe that since this is a new system, we should constantly examine what progress has been made in the development of the technique to see if changes in the system should be made.

I should admit at this point that this decision has not been an easy one. None of the great decisions made by a President are easy. But it is one that I have made after considering all of the options; and I would indicate, before going to your questions, two major options that I have overruled.

One is moving to a massive city defense. I have already indicated why I do not believe that is, first, feasible—and there is another reason: Moving to a massive city defense system, even starting with a thin system and then going to a heavy system, tends to be more provocative in terms of making credible a first-strike capability against the Soviet Union. I want no provocation which might deter arms talks.

The other alternative, at the other extreme, was to do nothing; or to delay for six or twelve months, which would be the equivalent, really, of doing nothing; or, for example, going the road only of research and development.

I have examined those options. I have ruled them out because I have concluded that the first deployment of this system, which will not occur until 1973—that that first deployment is essential by that date if we are to meet the threat that our present intelligence indicates will exist by 1973.

In other words, we must begin now. If we delay a year, for example, it means that that first deployment will be delayed until 1975. That might be too late.

It is the responsibility of the President of the United States, above all other responsibilities, to think first of the security of the United States. I believe that this system is the best step that we can take to provide for that security.

There are, of course, other possibilities that have been strongly urged by some of the leaders this morning: for example, that we could increase our offensive capability, our submarine force, or even our Minuteman force or our bomber force. That I would consider to be, however, the wrong road because it would be provocative to the Soviet Union and might escalate an arms race.

This system is truly a safeguard system, a defensive system only. It safeguards our deterrent and under those circumstances can in no way, in my opinion, delay the progress which I hope will continue to be made toward arms talks, which will limit arms, not only this kind of system but particularly offensive systems.

AN ARGUMENT AGAINST THE ABM [3]

JEROME B. WIESNER [4]

Some months before President Nixon decided in favor of the modified safeguard ABM system, the Center for the Study of Democratic Institutions conducted a conference in New York City at which four participants gave tightly reasoned cases for and against the construction and deployment of the antiballistic missile system. For the system were Donald Brennan, founder of the Hudson Institute, and Leon Johnson, former director of the Net Evaluation Subcommittee of the National Security Council. Presenting arguments against the proposal were Senator George S. McGovern of South Dakota and Jerome B. Wiesner.

The average citizen of our time is plainly incapable of understanding the scientific-technological intricacies of the missile defense systems. This is perhaps equally true of many of our leaders. Perhaps many of them would agree with C. P. Snow that at the highest level of administration decisions are often made "by men who cannot have a first-hand knowledge of what those choices depend upon or what their results may be." Accordingly, the officials who make what Tom Wicker of the New York *Times* has called "apocalyptic conclusions" must turn to their science advisers for much needed help. But scientific acumen and exacting analysis of data will not provide the final answer. Men must still make judgments, for these matters involve high moral considerations as well as scientific computation.

Dr. Wiesner's statement illustrates admirably the interaction of scientific knowledge and individual judgment in the assessment of a critical public issue. He brings impressive credentials to the symposium. With extensive experience in laboratory research, he has also served in high-level advisory capacities, notably as science and technology consultant to President John F. Kennedy, and is now provost of the Massachusetts Institute of Technology. His statement on the ABM was given in New York on November 19, 1968. Along with the other three presentations, it was an important

[3] Statement given at a conference of the Center for the Study of Democratic Institutions held in New York City, November 19, 1968. Text furnished by the Center; permission to reprint granted by Edward Reed, Director of Publications, Center for the Study of Democratic Institutions, Santa Barbara, California.

[4] For biographical note, see Appendix.

contribution to the understanding of an issue which could affect
the survival of the human race. Former Vice President Hubert H.
Humphrey put it clearly in January 1969 when he observed that
"no decision of the magnitude of ABM should be taken on . . .
[the American people's] behalf without greater evidence of their
informed consent than can be said to exist presently." Dr. Wiesner
provided an argument deserving of thoughtful analysis in this
continuing dialogue.

Dr. Karl Compton's sister, when living in India, watched
a handyman driving a nail in a wall of her house, tearing up
a lot of plaster in the process. In desperation, she finally
grabbed the hammer and nail and said: "My God, man, let
me do that. Why don't you use some common sense?" He
drew himself up in all his dignity and said: "Madam, common sense is a gift of God. I've only got a technical
education."

What I have found hardest to learn in twenty years of
dealing with military technology and international security
problems is how to add a measure of common sense to them.
Many other people have this problem, too. The whole issue
of ABM, I believe, ends up as a conflict of judgment rather
than one of analysis. Making the analysis is very important
because it provides the raw material for judgment; it gives
some feeling for what is possible and what isn't. But very
often it turns out that analyzing a complex situation offends
plain common sense or defies understanding. In studying a
complex problem like ABM, certain assumptions have to be
made, and if the assumptions are bad, the analysis will
simply conceal them.

This happens frequently, and is happening now in the
debates about the antiballistic missile. We do not have adequate knowledge about many aspects of an antiballistic missile duel because we lack vital data about the attacking missiles and about ABM performance. So we just pick some
numbers that seem rational and we use them to make whatever point serves our purpose.

I once had an argument with James Webb and his staff
about the best way to go to the moon. My calculations

showed that the lunar orbit approach was much less certain than the earth orbit estimates on which his reliability values for each operation were based—a prime example was the reliability of starting an engine. When he became convinced his conclusion was suspect, Mr. Webb set his analysts to work and they came back with some new figures that proved their point. Now, it was hard for me to judge whether the restart probability of an engine that had never been built was going to be .9997 or .99998. And it was numbers of this kind, by the computerful, that made the difference.

President Kennedy once said to me: "I don't understand. Scientists are supposed to be rational people. How can there be such differences on a technical issue?" I explained that it was nature that is rational, not the scientists, and that after scientists understand something they can explain nature rationally; when they attempt to evaluate something that has not been built, they have to make assumptions about what can be done, how fast it can be done, how well it is going to work, and what its effectiveness will be. Different people make different assumptions about all these elements. That is what is involved in the argument about antiballistic missile systems. One man's assumptions give one set of conclusions; another man's assumptions give a different set. Some of the assumptions are essentially undefinable—we are talking about things we do not and cannot know anything about, no matter how we try. And so you can take whichever set of assumptions you choose.

Of course, it gets even worse than that. When we design a system like the Sentinel and then analyze it, we assume almost idealized conditions. We assume it is going to work as specified, or we quite arbitrarily use some reliability estimate like .95. But we can't know whether that is even close to correct because we have never built or operated anything like the Sentinel before. Even though the Sentinel is a very simple system (compared to the one that some people would really like to build once they get the Sentinel under the tent), it is probably the most complicated electronic system anyone has ever tried to put together. Here it is, the most elaborate, sophisticated, dynamic combination of rocketry, radars, computers, electronics, and other technology ever proposed, and we are expecting that it will work and work well and not just well but perfectly the first time it is tried in a large-scale test. All kinds of mock tests can be invented for it, but the first genuine one will be when it is used in earnest. This contrasts with many weapons of the kind that were used in World War II, or now in Vietnam, where the soldiers must keep using them in spite of their defects until the military man understands their flaws and weaknesses and works his way around them, or, if they are too defective, he complains to the manufacturer and demands that they be straightened out. I would like to see the complaint the military writes to the manufacturer of the Sentinel system after it discovers that the computer program for discriminating between "garbage" and incoming nuclear warheads was written wrong, like the computer in the last election that reported that 180 per cent of the population of a particular town had voted.

In my opinion any ABM is untestable. I am offering you this as a judgment, not a technical fact. But I think it is something that ought to be kept in mind by anyone who is trying to understand the more detailed technical arguments.

To judge an ABM defense system we must know its purpose. Is it supposed to provide an area defense, or defense of missile sites, or defense of a fleet, or defense of a few cities? It has to have some specific purpose, but one of the interesting things about the argument for the ABM is that its purpose seems very hard to grasp. We were told at one point that the Sentinel system was intended to protect us against any irrational behavior on the part of the Chinese, though many people would contend that our existing deterrent system will do this adequately now. A careful analysis of the Sentinel system, however, does not show that Sentinel would provide protection against Chinese nuclear weapons for very long unless we make some unbelievably naïve assumptions about the Chinese—that they do not have access to our journals and

newspapers, for example, or that they are simply not thinking people.

I don't think we should spend much time talking about
the Sentinel. We ought to regard the Sentinel as a bad joke
perpetrated on us by Mr. McNamara and Mr. Johnson in an
election year. It seems to me that their very rationalization
—that it was to defend us against the Chinese but we would
stop building it if the Russians agreed not to build one—
demonstrates that well enough.

We should look at the more general question of large
antiballistic missile systems and concentrate on what the
military and the congressional enthusiasts for ABM would
like to build, if they could get us to agree. What they have in
mind is a much more sophisticated and elaborate antiballistic missile system that would have the capability of intercepting missiles fired at the United States. The question is: does
it make all that much difference to our security if an ABM
system can shoot down some fraction of the ballistic missiles
aimed at our cities? What, in fact, is the general, overall
effect on our security of creating an ABM system? How does
it change our deterrent posture? How much protection, if
any, will it give the country at large, or the military installations? What is its effect on our efforts to achieve a more
rational world? What does it do to a variety of other military
objectives we might have?

Before we approach such questions, there is one important
generalization I would like to stress, one that should always
be kept in mind while examining strategic-weapons systems
but that people almost always forget to take into account.
It is that these developments take a long time from conception to effective operational deployment. This gives a kind
of inherent stability to the character of the military-technical
race. To appreciate this fact, we need only to think back to
some of the frights that did not materialize—the missile gap
and the bomber gap, for example. It takes time and effort
to change the strategic balance drastically. The development
from the research stage, which itself takes time, to the proto-

type stage takes even more time, as do the testing and de-
bugging of anything so complicated. Engineering it into a
producible device takes more time, its production takes
time, its deployment into the field takes time. Finally it is
operational and then, if it is a defensive weapon, it is generally also obsolete. This whole cycle takes about ten years.

Some weapons systems are obsolete in their conception,
and I think this is probably true for the antiballistic missile
system before us. I have, in fact, come to the conclusion that
any system that depends on projectiles—rather than, say,
nuclear rays or electromagnetic beams or laser beams—is
futile.

In 1961, when President Kennedy first began to survey his
military problems, his attention was drawn forcefully to an
antimissile system, the Nike-Zeus. He began to get a flood of
mail, from friends, from Congress, from people in industry.
The press pointedly questioned him about his plans to deploy
the Nike-Zeus system. He began to see full-pages for it in
popular magazines like *Life* and *Saturday Evening Post*, proclaiming how Nike-Zeus would defend America, and listing
the industrial towns which would profit from the contracts
for it—advertisements, by the way, that were generally paid
for with government money as contract expenses. (The law
no longer permits such advertising to be charged to contracts.) This pressure built up to the point where President
Kennedy came to feel that the only thing anybody in the
country was concerned about was the Nike-Zeus. He began to
collect Nike-Zeus material. In one corner of a room he had
a pile of literature and letters and other materials on the
subject. He set out to make himself an expert on the Nike-
Zeus and spent hundreds of hours gathering views from the
scientific community about it. In the end he decided not to
deploy Nike-Zeus. Then something interesting happened. As
soon as the decision was made against Nike-Zeus, everybody
admitted that it was no good. People began to point out
weaknesses in the system—that, for example, it was a system
with very little discrimination between what it ought to in-

tercept and the decoys fired to confuse it. Even Mr. McNamara said that to have deployed the Nike-Zeus would have been a very serious mistake.

An antiballistic missile system attempts to intercept and destroy ballistic missiles coming in very fast, very high, from long distances. It requires that the defenders fire their own intercepting missiles from the ground after they have detected the incoming missiles with a long-range radar. Detection normally occurs when the attacking missiles are several hundred miles away if their trajectories are normal. They can be detected farther away if forward radars are employed. After detection one makes a rough projection or prediction of the trajectory of the incoming missile and launches an antimissile, usually a rocket carrying a nuclear warhead, in the direction of the incoming device. The missile-tracking radar on the ground must follow the incoming warhead and it tells the antimissile rocket where to go. When the defensive rocket gets close enough to the incoming missile its nuclear warhead is exploded and, in principle, destroys the attacking object. This has been demonstrated both by analysis and in field tests to be possible. No one questions that if you set up this kind of system it will work in an ideal situation.

However, there were several things wrong about the Nike-Zeus that would have made it relatively ineffective in real situations. First, as originally designed, it was supposed to intercept incoming missiles at very high altitudes, out of the atmosphere. This meant that it was easily confused; an enemy could mix real nuclear missiles with lightweight decoys made to look like missiles, and send them in against Nike-Zeus, so that it would be totally saturated. To correct this we allowed the incoming devices to come down into the atmosphere; the difference in weights allowed the heavy pieces, the real warheads, to go on, while all this other lightweight decoy junk was slowed down and separated out. This tended to work somewhat better, but even so the whole system, as conceived, really wasn't good enough. It could not respond fast enough. Its radars weren't good enough. Its traffic-handling capacity—that is, the number of missiles it could deal with at one time—was not adequate.

Also, Nike-Zeus was subject, as I believe all the later systems are, to something called blackout; that is, if a nuclear explosion were set off to destroy an incoming missile, it also upset the gas in the air, "ionized" it—electrons strip off from the molecules and for a while the gas acts like a metal rather than a gas so that radar waves cannot go through it and you cannot see what is behind it. Nike-Zeus was open to this in two ways. First, if you fired some rockets and they set off their own nuclear weapons, you might generate self-blackout. Second, if the enemy recognized that the defense had this vulnerability, he could design his offensive system to occasionally dump in a rocket with a nuclear warhead, explode it, and generate enough ionization to black out your radars. But Nike-Zeus had another interesting weakness—by the time it had been brought down to a reasonably low altitude so that the atmosphere would filter incoming devices, no one could be sure that when it set off its nuclear explosion it would not damage itself.

Nike-Zeus was a point defense system, and this posed two more problems. First, which points in the United States would be defended? This presented a terrible political problem. Would we defend the twenty-five largest cities? The fifty largest? Second, it was possible for an intelligent enemy to bypass the point defense system and land his nuclear weapons in the countryside, just outside the range of the system, generating a fallout attack on the population. This meant we would have to build fallout shelters on a grand scale.

As I said, once Nike-Zeus was turned off, even its strongest proponents admitted it had fatal weaknesses, and they undertook to try to fix them. The worst weaknesses of the Nike-Zeus have now been eliminated. The new system, Nike-X, of which the Sentinel uses some pieces—but which is certainly not what is being proposed as the full ABM to defend the United States—is improved in almost every aspect. Its radars are electrically scanned; they can look in all directions very rapidly. The radars have higher power so they can see farther. The Sentinel has two intercept rockets, one designed for low altitude, called Sprint, that can get up there fast and maneuver quickly; another called Spartan, for long-range interception. It has a computer system better able to discriminate between trash and nuclear warheads in the incoming package.

We have also changed, at least in principle, the way in which we would destroy incoming nuclear warheads. Still another problem with the Nike-Zeus was that its destruction of the incoming nuclear weapons depended on a phenomenon called neutron heating. When one explodes a nuclear weapon near another nuclear weapon, a flux of neutrons is released; these penetrate into the guts of the second nuclear weapon and heat it enough to melt it. However, this effect does not work over very great distances; so the Nike-Zeus presented us with the problem that a single defensive nuclear explosion could be effective against only a limited number of incoming missiles. Although I do not think that cost factors are the most important part of the argument, this did create an economic case against ABM.

Well, in Sentinel, at very high altitudes, we have gone over to another phenomenon called X-ray kill. We have substituted nuclear weapons that can generate an intense flux of X rays which are effective at greater distances than the neutrons. The difficulty with all of this is that it produces a kind of electronic Maginot Line. The defender sits and guesses about the attacker's tactics. If he guesses that one thing is going to happen, he invents a technology to deal with it. If he guesses that something else is going to happen, he invents another technology. But there is always the possibility that something quite unexpected will happen. I do not think the defender is ever going to know really what to expect; the variety of techniques available to a nation planning an offensive system is great enough to keep an antiballistic missile system of the kind we are talking about totally off balance.

As a matter of fact, just the thought that we might develop an antiballistic missile system, and therefore that the Russians might do the same thing, caused us to develop a whole new set of offensive countermeasures that make our Air Force and Navy confident that we do not have to worry about a Russian antimissile system. We have some new missiles that, instead of a single warhead, carry several and with high accuracy. We have available, and so do they, the possibility of using the blackout attack. One can develop very different kinds of offensive rockets that come in at low altitudes and do various elaborate maneuvers. We can shield against X rays. The choices are endless.

So, as I said in the beginning, anyone who makes calculations about what his defense system can do must make and proceed from a series of assumptions that do not seem to be warranted. But, of course, this does not stop people from making them.

In his 1967 "defense posture" speech, for example, former Defense Secretary McNamara cited some figures still widely quoted. He said a nuclear exchange with Russia in 1967 would cause 120 million American deaths. He then postulated two antimissile defense systems for the United States—one, Posture A, would cost $10 billion, and the other, Posture B, would cost $20 billion. His calculations indicated that the $10 billion system would reduce American fatalities to 40 million deaths, while the $20 billion system would reduce American fatalities to 30 million. These are numbers I find hard to grasp, but they obviously are meant to indicate a very substantial improvement in the fatality ratio if we were to build a defense system. However, more questions were left unanswered than were answered in the calculations. First, Mr. McNamara, I believe, assumed the system would work as planned. But, let me repeat, I have serious reservations about the effectiveness of such an ABM system even if a potential enemy were not devising things to undo its effectiveness. I do not think its performance would be anywhere near the advertised predictions because of its very complexity. Second, Mr. McNamara said he had made his calculations on the basis of the 1967 Soviet offensive missile deployment. But that was not a Soviet deployment the Russians told us about; it was only McNamara's guess, or somebody's guess, about the Soviet deployment. So our defense planners must have had to make certain assumptions not only about our own system's weakness and accuracy but also about how fast the Russian missiles would come in, how well they would be protected, and whether they would bear one warhead or two or more. Maybe Mr. McNamara knew all these things. But I suspect there were a lot of assumptions in his calculations that might not hold up. Even if they had held up in 1967 when they were made, I doubt that they would be of much use today.

Mr. McNamara said that the 1967 Soviet land-based missile force was 750 missiles and he estimated their future growth on a basis of past experience. I doubt if anyone today questions that the Soviet force is at least one third larger than it was in 1967; it grew much faster than predicted. So, even the simple estimate of the Soviet force was wrong. Furthermore, the United States could not have built the ABM system Mr. McNamara was talking about in the time available between 1967, when the calculation was made, and today. It would have taken five or six or seven years to build it. So Mr. McNamara would have had to have the nerve to guess what the Russian deployment would be in 1975 in order to have made a meaningful estimate for that time period. He obviously had sense enough not to try.

Unfortunately, many people do not read the fine print. They do not realize that you cannot snap your fingers and wish into existence that kind of antiballistic missile system being argued about. They do not realize that if we build an antiballistic missile system and the Russians regard it as something they do not like, they have plenty of time to respond and to figure out how to get their missiles past it, or that if they build an ABM system, we can respond in the same way.

In essence, then, my judgment is that we are just as likely to wind up a captive in the arms race if we start going the way of ABM defense as if we continue to build more and more offensive missiles.

There are people who say that it is better to spend your money on ABM defenses than on more destructive power. If one could do this—that is, freeze the offensive power on both sides and build only defensive systems—this might make ABM a good thing. If Congress, the military, and the manufacturers were happy to build only defenses and did not press us to add to the offensive forces, maybe ABM would be a good buy.

But I do not believe that this is a tenable situation, and this is the reason for one basic disagreement on the ABM. I think we would reach a point in the growth of the ABM defensive system where people would argue that improved defenses mean that the offenses no longer can guarantee deterrence and that we must therefore increase our offensive capability even more.

This is not a matter that anybody can settle with numbers and calculations. It is a judgment. But judgments of this kind are at the heart of the decision to build or not to build an ABM system, not the statistics, the calculations about "cost-effectiveness," or how many people will be killed. These factors are important in the decision, of course. What is most important, however, is the total dynamics and the likely interaction of the policymakers on both sides. I come back to where I began and ask: can we play this game, which certainly will not buy us real defense, and at the same time achieve a rational world? My answer is No.

And then I must add this last fillip to it: I believe that the situation will be made more, not less, dangerous. We always underestimate our own capabilities and overestimate that of the other fellow. I think this is true of both sides, and it generates what I call a parallax effect. That is, if the Russians build a defensive system, we think it is better than it is, so we overbuild in order to penetrate it, and vice versa.

Thus there is the real possibility that when everything is stabilized at some higher level and we are all relaxed because we have become used to it, the potential for destruction will have gone up instead of down.

REFLECTIONS ON WAR, PROTEST, AND THE GOVERNANCE OF MAN

A GENERATION IN SEARCH OF A FUTURE [1]

George Wald [2]

When Crocker Snow, Jr. and James G. Crowley, staff members of the Boston *Globe* returned from a meeting on March 4, 1969, in the Kresge Auditorium at the Massachusetts Institute of Technology, each reportedly said, independently of the other, "I think I've just listened to the most important speech of my lifetime." They were referring to the extemporaneous talk delivered by Dr. George Wald, Higgins Professor of Biology at Harvard University, before a meeting of teachers and students who were assessing certain of the ends which scientific information is currently serving. The Science Action Coordinating Committee and the Union of Concerned Scientists had conducted a "research stoppage" during the day. And according to the Boston *Globe*, the panels and talks were not coming off as well as had been expected. Apparently there was some restlessness among the twelve hundred persons in the hall when Dr. Wald took the floor. Suddenly the mood changed and in minutes he held the audience in rapt concern. At the end of his statement, he received "a prolonged standing ovation."

Dr. Wald's talk dealt with many themes, all interrelated. But the point of focus was student unrest. The volume of rhetoric on this subject has been considerable during the past eighteen months. Dissent and protest have been in the air. Confrontation between students and administrators has been commonplace. Additionally, civil disobedience, destruction of property, and violence have been widespread, both here and abroad. Critics of the social scene have in various ways probed the reasons for the upheavals. Some have tried to come up with solutions—occasionally in the face of coercive threats—that would help restore the colleges and universities as centers of free and rational inquiry. At best, the efforts at restoration have not been uniformly successful, and in certain respects

---

[1] Address delivered at the Kresge Auditorium, Massachusetts Institute of Technology, March 4, 1969. Text furnished by WGBH-FM, Boston, from its radio recording of the address. Permission to reprint granted by Dr. Wald and WGBH-FM, Boston.

[2] For biographical note, see Appendix.

conditions have worsened over the past six months. Grievances, frustrations, and injustices of long standing have not yielded swiftly to correction; and the resulting impatience has often prompted the protesters to direct and disruptive actions. Apart from some of the disorder which appeared theatrically revolutionary, there was a complex cluster of reasons which drove many young people to search fiercely for new values and goals which, they hoped, would offer greater promise not only to themselves but to the community of man.

In the speech below, Nobel prizewinner George Wald tried, in a sort of wide-ranging testament, to pin down some of the reasons for the uneasiness of the younger generation. It is a rather remarkable speech both in scope and expression, and so adjudged even by critics who disagree vigorously—even angrily—with its theses and its logic. The text has been widely circulated: originally in the Boston *Globe,* which printed the full text from the tape recording furnished by WGBH, Channel 2; in the *New Yorker,* which on March 22 quoted at length from the text; in the *Congressional Record*; and subsequently in many newspapers throughout the country. It deserves a wide reading, a careful reading, for within its compass is an agenda of human imperatives with which both young and old must deal if, as Dr. Wald said, we are not "to go down in history as the apocalyptic generation." Perhaps the cure for student unrest is, as Dr. Wald wrote afterward, *adult* unrest. "Produce enough adult unrest," he remarked, and students "will be glad to stay in their classes, getting ready to live in that better world that we adults are preparing for them."

All of you know that in the last couple of years there has been student unrest breaking at times into violence in many parts of the world: in England, Germany, Italy, Spain, Mexico and, needless to say, in many parts of this country. There has been a great deal of discussion as to what it all means. Perfectly clearly it means something different in Mexico from what it does in France, and something different in France from what it does in Tokyo, and something different in Tokyo from what it does in this country. Yet unless we are to assume that students have gone crazy all over the world, or that they have just decided that it's the thing to do, there must be some common meaning.

I don't need to go so far afield to look for that meaning. I am a teacher, and at Harvard, I have a class of about 350 students—men and women—most of them freshmen and sophomores. Over these past few years I have felt increasingly that something is terribly wrong—and this year ever so much more than last. Something has gone sour, in teaching and in learning. It's almost as though there were a widespread feeling that education has become irrelevant.

A lecture is much more of a dialogue than many of you probably appreciate. As you lecture, you keep watching the faces; and information keeps coming back to you all the time. I began to feel, particularly this year, that I was missing much of what was coming back. I tried asking the students, but they didn't or couldn't help me very much.

But I think I know what's the matter, even a little better than they do. I think that this whole generation of students is beset with a profound uneasiness. I don't think that they have yet quite defined its source, I think I understand the reasons for their uneasiness even better than they do. What is more, I share their uneasiness.

What's bothering those students? Some of them tell you it's the Vietnam war. I think the Vietnam war is the most shameful episode in the whole of American history. The concept of War Crimes is an American invention. We've committed many War Crimes in Vietnam; but I'll tell you something interesting about that. We were committing War Crimes in World War II, even before Nuremburg trials were held and the principle of War Crimes started. The saturation bombing of German cities was a War Crime. Dropping atom bombs on Hiroshima and Nagasaki was a War Crime. If we had lost the war, some of our leaders might have had to answer for those actions.

I've gone through all of that history lately, and I find that there's a gimmick in it. It isn't written out, but I think we established it by precedent. That gimmick is that if one can allege that one is repelling or retaliating for an aggression—after that everything goes. And you see we are living in a world in which all wars are wars of defense. All War Departments are now Defense Departments. This is all part of the double-talk of our time. The aggressor is always on the other side. And I suppose this is why our ex-Secretary of State, Dean Rusk—a man in whom repetition takes the place of reason, and stubbornness takes the place of character—went to such pains to insist, as he still insists, that in Vietnam we are repelling an aggression. And if that's what we are doing—so runs the doctrine—anything goes. If the concept of War Crimes is ever to mean anything, they will have to be defined as categories of acts, regardless of alleged provocation. But that isn't so now.

I think we've lost that war, as a lot of other people think, too. The Vietnamese have a secret weapon. It's their willingness to die, beyond our willingness to kill. In effect they've been saying, you can kill us, but you'll have to kill a lot of us, you may have to kill all of us. And thank heavens, we are not yet ready to do that.

Yet we have come a long way—far enough to sicken many Americans, far enough even to sicken our fighting men. Far enough so that our national symbols have gone sour. How many of you can sing about "the rockets' red glare, bombs bursting in air" without thinking, those are *our* bombs and *our* rockets bursting over South Vietnamese villages? When those words were written, we were a people struggling for freedom against oppression. Now we are supporting real or thinly disguised military dictatorships all over the world, helping them to control and repress peoples struggling for their freedom.

But that Vietnam war, shameful and terrible as it is, seems to me only an immediate incident in a much larger and more stubborn situation.

Part of my trouble with students is that almost all the students I teach were born since World War II. Just after World War II, a series of new and abnormal procedures came into American life. We regarded them at the time as temporary aberrations. We thought we would get back to normal American life some day. But those procedures have stayed with us now for more than twenty years, and those students of mine have never known anything else. They think those things are normal. They think we've always had a Pentagon, that we have always had a big army, and that we always had a draft. But those are all new things in American life; and I think that they are incompatible with what America meant before.

How many of you realize that just before World War II the entire American army, including the Air Force, numbered 139,000 men? Then World War II started, but we weren't yet in it; and seeing that there was great trouble in the world, we doubled this army to 268,000 men. Then in World War II it got to be 8 million. And then World War II came to an end, and we prepared to go back to a peacetime army somewhat as the American army had always been before. And indeed in 1950—you think about 1950, our international commitments, the Cold War, the Truman Doctrine, and all the rest of it—in 1950 we got down to 600,000 men.

Now we have 3.5 million men under arms: about 600,000 in Vietnam, about 300,000 more in "support areas" elsewhere in the Pacific, about 250,000 in Germany. And there are a lot at home. Some months ago we were told that 300,000 National Guardsmen and 200,000 reservists—so half a million men—had been specially trained for riot duty in the cities.

I say the Vietnam war is just an immediate incident, because so long as we keep that big an army, it will always find things to do. If the Vietnam war stopped tomorrow, with that big a military establishment the chances are that we would be in another such adventure abroad or at home before you knew it.

As for the draft: Don't reform the draft—get rid of it.

A peacetime draft is the most un-American thing I know. All the time I was growing up I was told about oppressive Central European countries and Russia, where young men were forced into the army; and I was told what they did about it. They chopped off a finger, or shot off a couple of toes; or better still, if they could manage it, they came to this country. And we understood that, and sympathized, and were glad to welcome them.

Now by present estimates four to six thousand Americans of draft age have left this country for Canada, another two or three thousand have gone to Europe, and it looks as though many more are preparing to emigrate.

A few months ago I received a letter from the *Harvard Alumni Bulletin* posing a series of questions that students might ask a professor involving what to do about the draft. I was asked to write what I would tell those students. All I had to say to those students was this: If any of them had decided to evade the draft and asked my help, I would help him in any way I could. I would feel as I suppose members of the underground railway felt in pre-Civil War days, helping runaway slaves to get to Canada. It wasn't altogether a popular position then; but what do you think of it now?

A bill to stop the draft was recently introduced in the Senate (S. 503), sponsored by a group of senators that ran the gamut from McGovern and Hatfield to Barry Goldwater. I hope it goes through; but any time I find that Barry Goldwater and I are in agreement, that makes me take another look.

And indeed there are choices in getting rid of the draft. I think that when we get rid of the draft, we must also cut back the size of the armed forces. It seems to me that in peacetime a total of one million men is surely enough. If there is an argument for American military forces of more than one million men in peacetime, I should like to hear that argument debated.

There is another thing being said closely connected with this: that to keep an adequate volunteer army, one would have to raise the pay considerably. That's said so positively and often that people believe it. I don't think it is true.

The great bulk of our present armed forces are genuine volunteers. Among first-term enlistments, 49 per cent are true volunteers. Another 30 per cent are so-called "reluctant volunteers," persons who volunteer under pressure of the draft.

Only 21 per cent are draftees. All reenlistments, of course, are true volunteers.

So the great majority of our present armed forces are true volunteers. Whole services are composed entirely of volunteers: the Air Force for example, the Navy, almost all the Marines. That seems like proof to me that present pay rates are adequate. One must add that an Act of Congress in 1967 raised the base pay throughout the services in three installments, the third installment still to come, on April 1, 1969. So it is hard to understand why we are being told that to maintain adequate armed services on a volunteer basis will require large increases in pay; they will cost an extra $17 billion per year. It seems plain to me that we can get all the armed forces we need as volunteers, and at present rates of pay.

But there is something ever so much bigger and more important than the draft. That bigger thing, of course, is what ex-President Eisenhower warned us of, calling it the military-industrial complex. I am sad to say that we must begin to think of it now as the military-industrial-labor union complex. What happened under the plea of the Cold War was not alone that we built up the first big peacetime army in our history, but we institutionalized it. We built, I suppose, the biggest government building in our history to run it, and we institutionalized it.

I don't think we can live with the present military establishment and its $80-billion-a-year budget, and keep America anything like we have known it in the past. It is corrupting the life of the whole country. It is buying up everything in sight: industries, banks, investors, universities; and lately it seems also to have bought up the labor unions.

The Defense Department is always broke; but some of the things they do with that $80 billion a year would make Buck Rogers envious. For example: the Rocky Mountain Arsenal on the outskirts of Denver was manufacturing a deadly nerve poison on such a scale that there was a problem of waste disposal. Nothing daunted, they dug a tunnel two

miles deep under Denver, into which they have injected so
much poisoned water that beginning a couple of years ago
Denver began to experience a series of earth tremors of increasing severity. Now there is a grave fear of a major earth-
quake. An interesting debate is in progress as to whether
Denver will be safer if that lake of poisoned water is removed
or left in place. (New York *Times,* July 4, 1968; *Science,*
September 27, 1968)

Perhaps you have read also of those 6,000 sheep that suddenly died in Skull Valley, Utah, killed by another nerve
poison—a strange and, I believe, still unexplained accident,
since the nearest testing seems to have been thirty miles away.

As for Vietnam, the expenditure of fire power has been
frightening. Some of you may still remember Khe Sanh, a
hamlet just south of the Demilitarized Zone, where a force
of United States Marines was beleaguered for a time. During
that period we dropped on the perimeter of Khe Sanh more
explosives than fell on Japan throughout World War II, and
more than fell on the whole of Europe during the years
1942 and 1943.

One of the officers there was quoted as having said afterward, "It looks like the world caught smallpox and died."
(New York *Times,* March 28, 1968)

The only point of government is to safeguard and foster
life. Our government has become preoccupied with death,
with the business of killing and being killed. So-called Defense now absorbs 60 per cent of the national budget, and
about 12 per cent of the gross national product.

A lively debate is beginning again on whether or not we
should deploy antiballistic missiles, the ABM. I don't have
to talk about them, everyone else here is doing that. But I
should like to mention a curious circumstance. In September,
1967, or about one and a half years ago, we had a meeting of
MIT and Harvard people, including experts on these matters, to talk about whether anything could be done to block
the Sentinel system, the deployment of ABM's. Everyone
present thought them undesirable; but a few of the most

knowledgeable persons took what seemed to be the practical view, "Why fight about a dead issue? It has been decided, the funds have been appropriated. Let's go on from there."

Well, fortunately, it's not a dead issue.

An ABM is a nuclear weapon. It takes a nuclear weapon to stop a nuclear weapon. And our concern must be with the whole issue of nuclear weapons.

There is an entire semantics ready to deal with the sort of thing I am about to say. It involves such phrases as "those are the facts of life." No—these are the facts of death. I don't accept them, and I advise you not to accept them. We are under repeated pressures to accept things that are presented to us as settled—decisions that have been made. Always there is the thought: let's go on from there! But this time we don't see how to go on. We will have to stick with those issues.

We are told that the United States and Russia between them have by now stockpiled in nuclear weapons approximately the explosive power of fifteen tons of TNT for every man, woman and child on earth. And now it is suggested that we must make more. All very regrettable, of course; but those are "the facts of life." We really would like to disarm; but our new Secretary of Defense has made the ingenious proposal that now is the time to greatly increase our nuclear armaments so that we can disarm from a position of strength.

I think all of you know there is no adequate defense against massive nuclear attack. It is both easier and cheaper to circumvent any known nuclear defense system than to provide it. It's all pretty crazy. At the very moment we talk of deploying ABM's, we are also building the MIRV, the weapon to circumvent ABM's.

So far as I know, the most conservative estimates of Americans killed in a major nuclear attack with everything working as well as can be hoped and all foreseeable precautions taken, run to about 50 millions. We have become callous to gruesome statistics, and this seems at first to be only another gruesome statistic. You think, Bang!—and next morning, if you're still there, you read in the newspapers that 50 million people were killed.

But that isn't the way it happens. When we killed close to 200,000 people with those first little, old-fashioned uranium bombs that we dropped on Hiroshima and Nagasaki, about the same number of persons was maimed, blinded, burned, poisoned and otherwise doomed. A lot of them took a long time to die.

That's the way it would be. Not a bang, and a certain number of corpses to bury; but a nation filled with millions of helpless, maimed, tortured and doomed persons, and the survivors huddled with their families in shelters, with guns ready to fight off their neighbors, trying to get some uncontaminated food and water.

A few months ago Senator Richard Russell of Georgia ended a speech in the Senate with the words: "If we have to start over again with another Adam and Eve, I want them to be Americans; and I want them on this continent and not in Europe." That was a United States senator holding a patriotic speech. Well, here is a Nobel Laureate who thinks that those words are criminally insane. [Prolonged applause.]

How real is the threat of full-scale nuclear war? I have my own very inexpert idea, but realizing how little I know and fearful that I may be a little paranoid on this subject, I take every opportunity to ask reputed experts. I asked that question of a very distinguished professor of government at Harvard about a month ago. I asked him what sort of odds he would lay on the possibility of full-scale nuclear war within the foreseeable future. "Oh," he said comfortably, "I think I can give you a pretty good answer to that question. I estimate the probability of full-scale nuclear war, provided that the situation remains about as it is now, at 2 per cent per year." Anybody can do the simple calculation that shows that 2 per cent per year means that the chance of having that full-scale nuclear war by 1990 is about one in three, and by 2000 it is about 50-50.

I think I know what is bothering the students. I think that what we are up against is a generation that is by no means sure that it has a future.

I am growing old, and my future so to speak is already behind me. But there are those students of mine who are in my mind always; and there are my children, two of them now seven and nine, whose future is infinitely more precious to me than my own. So it isn't just their generation; it's mine too. We're all in it together.

Are we to have a chance to live? We don't ask for prosperity, or security; only for a reasonable chance to live, to work out our destiny in peace and decency. Not to go down in history as the apocalyptic generation.

And it isn't only nuclear war. Another overwhelming threat is in the population explosion. That has not yet even begun to come under control. There is every indication that the world population will double before the year 2000; and there is a widespread expectation of famine on an unprecedented scale in many parts of the world. The experts tend to differ only in their estimates of when those famines will begin. Some think by 1980, others think they can be staved off until 1990, very few expect that they will not occur by the year 2000.

That is the problem. Unless we can be surer than we now are that this generation has a future, nothing else matters. It's not good enough to give it tender loving care, to supply it with breakfast foods, to buy it expensive educations. Those things don't mean anything unless this generation has a future. And we're not sure that it does.

I don't think that there are problems of youth, or student problems. All the real problems I know are grown-up problems.

Perhaps you will think me altogether absurd, or "academic," or hopelessly innocent—that is, until you think of the alternatives—if I say as I do to you now: we have to get rid of those nuclear weapons. There is nothing worth having that can be obtained by nuclear war: nothing material or ideological, no tradition that it can defend. It is utterly self-defeating. Those atom bombs represent an unusable weapon. The only use for an atom bomb is to keep somebody else from using it. It can give us no protection, but only the doubtful satisfaction of retaliation. Nuclear weapons offer us nothing but a balance of terror; and a balance of terror is still terror.

We have to get rid of those atomic weapons, here and everywhere. We cannot live with them.

I think we've reached a point of great decision, not just for our nation, not only for all humanity, but for life upon the earth. I tell my students, with a feeling of pride that I hope they will share, that the carbon, nitrogen and oxygen that make up 99 per cent of our living substance, were cooked in the deep interiors of earlier generations of dying stars. Gathered up from the ends of the universe, over billions of years, eventually they came to form in part the substance of our sun, its planets and ourselves. Three billion years ago life arose upon the earth. It seems to be the only life in the solar system. Many a star has since been born and died.

About two million years ago, man appeared. He has become the dominant species on the earth. All other living things, animal and plant, live by his sufferance. He is the custodian of life on earth. It's a big responsibility.

The thought that we're in competition with Russians or with Chinese is all a mistake, and trivial. Only mutual destruction lies that way. We are one species, with a world to win. There's life all over this universe, but in all the universe we are the only men.

Our business is with life, not death. Our challenge is to give what account we can of what becomes of life in the solar system, this corner of the universe that is our home and, most of all, what becomes of men—all men of all nations, colors and creeds. It has become one world, a world for all men. It is only such a world that now can offer us life and the chance to go on.

MARTIN LUTHER KING AND
AMERICAN TRADITIONS [3]

JOHN HOPE FRANKLIN [4]

On April 4, 1968, Dr. Martin Luther King, Jr., was assassi-
nated. Five days later, his close friend, Dr. Benjamin E. Mays,
president emeritus of Morehouse College, delivered the eloquent
eulogy which was reprinted in REPRESENTATIVE AMERICAN SPEECHES:
1967-1968. In 1963 Dr. King had revealed the dimensions of his
dream for America in a celebrated speech which is already firmly
fixed in the literature of great American oratory. Dr. Mays spoke
of the dramatic impact of that dream and of the influence it
exerted upon America and the world. He closed by expressing
what Dr. King believed: "If physical death was the price he had
to pay to rid America of prejudice and injustice, nothing could
be more redemptive."

Now, one year later, another eloquent man has spoken on
the state of Dr. King's dream and has concluded, sadly, that it is
not moving toward fulfillment, nor, in fact, is there "a national
resolve to work at it." Said John Hope Franklin:

> What national anguish his death brought was short-lived,
> if indeed it existed at all. We do not seem to have moved
> significantly toward the goals he sought or even in the
> direction of those goals. There has been no large enlistment
> of Americans in the causes for which he gave his life, no
> greater national resolve to finish the task of creating a decent
> social order.

Dr. Franklin, chairman of the history department at the University of Chicago, delivered the address at a memorial service at
the Department of Labor in Washington, D.C., on April 4, 1969.

Students of oratory will be interested in another of Dr.
Franklin's recent speeches, "The American Scholar and American
Foreign Policy." It contains a distinctive development of the
scholar-statesman theme which has its roots in the early addresses

---

[3] Address delivered at a memorial service at the Department of Labor,
Washington, D.C., April 4, 1969. Text furnished by Dr. Franklin, with permission for this reprint.

[4] For biographical note, see Appendix.

of William Tyrell Channing and Ralph Waldo Emerson. An
adaptation of Dr. Franklin's address appeared in *The American
Scholar,* Autumn 1968, pages 615-623.

Some years ago, when the Congress of the United States
was considering a civil rights bill, a young black man—not
yet thirty years of age—spoke out vigorously and eloquently
in support of the bill. Referring to the numerous forms of
injustice and discrimination from which his people suffered,
he said, "If this unjust discrimination is to be longer toler-
ated by the American people . . . then I can only say with
sorrow and regret that our boasted civilization is a fraud;
our republican institutions a failure; our social system a dis-
grace; and our religion a complete hypocrisy." The speaker
was John R. Lynch, a member of the House of Representatives from Mississippi; and he was urging his colleagues in
1875 to put an end to racial discrimination in the public
schools, on the railroads, and in other places of public
accommodation.

Congress passed the act after five years of debate and after
deleting the provision covering the public schools. A few
years later the Supreme Court struck down the law, with the
neat but unconvincing remark that the law to protect the
civil rights of all people had not been authorized by the
Constitution. The decision was hailed throughout the land
as a just decision. Whites in the South praised the "fair-
mindedness" of the Court in striking down the work of a "set
of political fanatics." A New York newspaper advised Negroes to "act wisely" and "accept the result with patience."
Only Negro Americans and a very few white Americans deplored the decision. T. Thomas Fortune said that his fellow
blacks felt as if they had been "baptized in ice water." Frederick Douglass, commenting on the ultimate indivisibility of
justice, observed that under the circumstances the wife of the
Chief Justice was protected "not by law, but solely by the
accident of her color. . . . The lesson of all the ages on this
point is that a wrong done to one man is a wrong done to

all men. It may not be felt at the moment . . . but . . . the harvest of evil will come."

Thus began the third century of racial injustice in the New World utopia. Those earlier years—from the seventeenth to the nineteenth centuries—had been marked not merely by the barbarism of slavery but also by the denial of equal rights to those blacks who were already free. Those earlier years had witnessed the struggle of white Americans to win their political independence and their simultaneous determination to deny even the rudiments of freedom to their black compatriots who had also fought to make the country strong and free. Long before the great numbers of Europeans had poured into the American cities, white America had developed the fine art of ghettoizing the American urban community by placing beyond the pale those Negroes who lived in eighteenth century Boston, New York, and Philadelphia. And when, in the ripeness of time, the United States found it necessary to fight to save its own life, it faltered time and again between 1861 and 1865 on the fundamental questions of human freedom and the dignity of all men.

But it was in this third century—these last hundred years —that this country, through its laws and its practices, would formalize, institutionalize, and even intellectualize its racial doctrines. It would segregate its labor force on the basis of race. Race would dictate the separation of the armed forces into white and black outfits that would fight separately to save the world for democracy. The etiquette of race relations would require separate housing, separate entrances and exits in buildings, separate public parks, separate schools, separate churches, separate toilets, separate Bibles on which to take the oath in courts of law, separate telephone booths, separate drinking fountains, and separate warehouses for the storing of school books of white and black children. Segregation would encourage and justify discrimination. Discrimination would facilitate the brutalizing and dehumanizing of an entire race. The doctrine of racial inferiority, deeply embedded in the very ethos of white America by three centuries of preaching, would rationalize every act of bestiality perpetrated against black men by white Americans.

By the time that Martin Luther King appeared on the American scene in the middle of the twentieth century, American attitudes toward race had hardened into a firm doctrine of racism that pervaded every aspect of American life. It had itself become a powerful American tradition, even if it was not a good American tradition. It must have been a painful sight for a man such as Martin Luther King, deeply committed to a life of love, to view a society so committed to the denial of equality. Even though he admonished his followers to love their enemies—"and let them know that you love them," he would say—he was doubtless hurt by the regular and persistent reciprocation of hate. But this was an old American tradition, this blind hatred, with a basis so ephemeral as color and employing violence whenever necessary to preserve the tradition; and Martin Luther King knew his history as well as his theology. He knew how far back race hatred went, how deeply it was embedded, how pervasive it was. He would confront this tradition, and he would give his entire life to its obliteration.

There were other powerful American traditions on which King could rely as he fought the tradition of racism in all its forms. One was the tradition of protest—to be sure, not always as peaceful in the past as King would have liked, but sanctified by the constitutional provision guaranteeing the "right of the people peaceably to assemble and to petition the government for a redress of grievances." If Patrick Henry could cry "Give me liberty or give me death," when England imposed a stamp tax, surely King could protest the indignities heaped on his people by forcing them to enter a bus by a rear door. If Henry David Thoreau could denounce the Commonwealth of Massachusetts for enacting laws that interfered with his complete freedom, surely King could protest the failure of the Federal Government to protect black citizens against the dogs, fire hoses, and bull whips of the racist keepers of the peace. If women could protest in every conceivable way the inequalities of the sexes, surely King could protest the discriminations in employment, housing, voting, and education.

And so Martin Luther King embraced the great American tradition of protest, rejecting that portion of it that countenanced violence. For his efforts he was jailed, an eventuality that he invited *and* expected in order to test what he viewed as unjust and unconstitutional laws. For his efforts he was denounced as "communistic" by a southern newspaper and was called "the most notorious liar in the country" by the director of the FBI. This, too, he accepted with equanimity, realizing that in the heat of the battle for justice, men become desperate when their defenses become weak. But he could not and would not accept the violence and barbarity of his adversaries who could bomb scores of churches where defenseless Negroes met to protest injustices, who could murder men and women whose only crime as they worked in the field of civil rights was their search for decency, who could murder little children whose only offense was that they attended Sunday School. His adversaries had taken that part of the American tradition that he had rejected and with it they had defamed and defiled a cause that was worthy and just.

He was not daunted, however, for his optimism was boundless; and his faith in the ultimate triumph of his cause was unshakable. Long before the President's Advisory Commission on Civil Disorders made its report, King knew and had said that racism was deeply embedded in the vital organs of American life; but he believed that it could be uprooted. He had seen hatred, and he had seen violence; but he believed that there was enough decency left that could be aroused and used to dispel those forces that were on the verge of destroying the country. He believed that a combination of Christian militancy and the American concept of equality could strengthen each other and, in the process, could indeed overcome the forces of evil. He had said as much in his "Letter from a Birmingham Jail." He was to say it again in his book, *Why We Can't Wait.*

There was yet another American tradition on which Martin Luther King counted and of which he became a part. It was the tradition of the Negro American serving as the corrective to the one-sided, myopic view of justice so often manifested by white Americans, even in their finest hour. When they were fighting for independence against England, it was the Negroes of Massachusetts who reminded them of their inconsistency, if not their hypocrisy, in keeping black men in bondage while espousing the cause of freedom. It was a voteless black man, Paul Cuffe, who refused to pay his taxes and went to jail in 1780 in order to point up the shallow speciousness of the claim of the patriots that "taxation without representation is tyranny." It was Frederick Douglass who reminded President Lincoln that the cause of Union was tenuous and uncertain so long as slavery, the cause of the Civil War, was permitted to exist. It was a company of black Union soldiers who, in 1865, told President Andrew Johnson that it was strange that former Confederates, returning from doing battle *against* the Union for four years, were allowed to vote while Negro soldiers who had fought to *save* the Union were denied the vote, presumably because they did not possess the qualities of mind and the powers of discrimination to understand the problems of the society.

This was, indeed, a great American tradition; and one wonders how the country could have retained its sanity or its soul without it. It sustained a country virtually gone mad, at the turn of the century, as it glorified segregation, discrimination, lynchings, and rioting. A T. Thomas Fortune, a Monroe Trotter, and a W. E. B. Du Bois spoke gently to the conscience of the nation and reminded it that it was supposed to be a civilized society and should act like one. When this country embarked on a war to save the world for democracy and sent a racially segregated army overseas to fight that war, only Negro Americans pointed out the awkwardness and the incongruity of such a posture. It was Negro

Americans who first suggested that the disingenuous doctrine of separate but equal not only insulted the Constitution but blasphemed the human spirit as well. It was a difficult task always to be pointing out inconsistencies, pleading for an end to hypocrisy, calling on the great democratic nation to correct its own weaknesses, but they faced the task and tried to discharge it not merely for their own sake but for the sake of their country.

And now, in the middle of the twentieth century, it was the task of young Martin Luther King to reach back through the years and join with young John R. Lynch, who fought for civil rights in 1875, and to join with the countless Negro Americans who, for centuries, had kept alive the tradition of trying to endow this nation with a soul. It was a rich tradition and a formidable task from which King did not shrink. For almost fifteen years, his voice was the world's most eloquent voice to speak for all mankind. And he worked as hard as he spoke: for an end to suffering in Nigeria, for the eradication of slums in urban America, for equal justice under law, for equality in employment, housing, and educational opportunities, for decency in all human relations, for peace at home and in the world.

Then, in the midst of his efforts—and before this nation could fully understand the meaning of his life and work— he had fallen. In death he was the victim of one of America's strongest and most enduring traditions, that of violence. The sniper, in a very real way, symbolized the mood of the nation: an unwillingness and a lack of courage to face the problems that Martin Luther King worked so hard to solve. The murderer was too cowardly to confront King and argue against his program of justice and brotherhood; and so he resorted to violence, the easy way out. For three centuries this nation had lacked the courage to face up to its racial problems. Instead of facing them in King's time, it sought to rationalize, justify, and even defend its own derelictions. Those who sought fair employment were branded as dupes of the Communist conspiracy, while the victims of discrimination in employment continued to go hungry. Those who sought better schools in the ghetto were being used, so the argument went, by the anarchists and others who did not care for the American way. As a nation we have been too cowardly to face the issues; it has been much easier to snipe at the advocates of change.

At the time of King's death a year ago, a great deal was said about the meaning of his life and the possible impact of his death on the causes for which he fought. It was even suggested that perhaps he achieved in his martyrdom what he could not achieve in life: a national sense of outrage against violence as well as injustice, and a national commitment, at long last, to attack the race problem with resources as well as resolution. This was, of course, a misreading of the national mood. Some mourned his death; others were elated. Some children in an Alabama town were taught to rejoice in his death. In a score of cities across the land even many of his own despairing followers forgot the teachings of their leader and vented their outrage in a thousand senseless acts of violence. In a Chicago suburb a white family was hounded out of town because they flew their flag at half-mast on the day of King's funeral.

The nation's flags were officially at half-mast, but there was yet no indication that the dream of Martin Luther King would be fulfilled or that there was a national resolve to work at it. It was a simple dream—that men shall dwell in peace and mutual respect. The dream would not come true simply because a few of the wealthy spent the Monday following his death washing windows in the ghetto and then retreated into their own gilded ghetto, satisfied with the penance they had done. It would not come true so long as the nation expended more of its resources and energies on the shot to the moon than on hunger and disease in American communities. It would not come true so long as companies that select their employees on the irrelevant basis of race receive favors and contracts from the Government that is supposed to be the Government of all the people. The dream of Martin Luther King would not come true so long as the nation drained its resources and offered the flower of its manhood in a war that few people fully countenanced or understood. And his dream turns into a nightmare with the realization that in Germany, Korea, Vietnam, and elsewhere, white American soldiers and black American soldiers do battle with one another and contribute to that polarization of the races of which King despaired.

And surely the dream of Martin Luther King would not come true if the trial of his accused assassin were permitted to sink into a mockery of the administration of justice. With good reason Negro Americans have always believed that justice in the United States was neither evenhanded nor color-blind. They had early fallen victims of two sets of laws—one for whites and one for blacks. Then they had seen the highest courts of the land sanction laws that made racial distinctions. They had seen the courts turn their backs on discrimination in so sacred an exercise of citizenship as voting. They were, thus, fully prepared to believe, on the basis of their long, agonizing experience with law and justice, that King's murderer would *not* come to trial and be judged on the basis of the evidence. How were they to know that he would be tried, convicted, sentenced, and imprisoned—all within twenty-four hours—with a thousand unanswered questions including the one raised by the prisoner himself that clearly implied the existence of a conspiracy. It was enough to shake the faith of *any* American. It was too much to ask black Americans to have faith in this bizarre administration of American justice where so little faith already existed.

On the first anniversary of the death of Martin Luther King, it is fitting that we search for some meaning for us of his life and death. It is no easy task. We lack perspective; our emotions betray us. A few things seem clear, however. What national anguish his death brought was short-lived, if indeed it existed at all. We do not seem to have moved significantly toward the goals he sought or even in the direction of those goals. There has been no large enlistment of Americans in the causes for which he gave his life, no great national resolve to finish the task of creating a decent social order.

But his death can be viewed as a warning that the time is running out when we can solve any of our major problems peacefully. The violent death of a man of peace triggered a period of convulsive and tragic violence. It provided yet another example of America's living and dying by the sword. The strain on our legal and political institutions of the murder of a President, and then a great national leader, and then a United States Senator is incalculable. It pushes us closer to the brink of anarchy; and the alarming deterioration of the rule of law is surely related to these violent and untimely deaths.

A young nation, once the hope of the old world and the new, grows old and weary before its time. It seems unable to cope with the forces that propel it toward its own demise. It is the nature of its own life that has done this to it. A nation cannot be profligate and incontinent in its regard for its own people without draining itself of its own vitality as well as its own humanity. Perhaps it can recover, but not without some strong resolve—stronger than anything we have yet witnessed—to become the vessel in which the lives and hopes of all its people can flourish and thereby bring about the restoration of its own vitality. Is this requiring too much?

When a young poet of another nation learned of the death of Martin Luther King, he wrote:

> That bullet killed him,
> but by that bullet I was reborn,
> and I was reborn a Negro.

No one requires that of any nation, surely not *this* nation; but those lines may contain the key to our salvation. If the death of Martin Luther King can, somehow, mean that the nation will experience a rebirth of simple humanity, then it can save itself and all of his dreams can then come true.

DARKNESS OVER THE IVORY TOWER [5]

MALCOLM MOOS [6]

If the pattern of life is etched by repetition and refrain, the features of campus unrest should by this time be unmistakably clear. During the past year, no subject—with the exception of Vietnam—has been more widely discussed, publicized, and assessed. The dimensions of student protest have been extensive, ranging from dissent in the best democratic tradition to open violence and take-over. All motivations for the demonstrations aside, the hard fact remains that the institutions of higher learning are beleaguered, and the end is seemingly not yet in sight.

The campus uprisings have produced a wide variety of rhetorical displays: fiery impromptu calls for immediate action, somewhat less impassioned appeals for moderation, and reasoned confrontations in search of solutions to alleged or real wrongs. In some instances, coercive force has played a part in the transactions. But whether raw force is an aspect of the process of persuasion is arguable. Admittedly, it is a means of social control, but that does not automatically make it a persuasive instrument providing freedom of choice from a list of reasoned alternatives.

Much of the dissatisfaction and anger vented on the colleges and universities is understandable, and reasoned dissent is a proper method of seeking correction. But the condition which prompts much unrest goes far beyond the boundaries of the campus; it affects the entire society and culture. The colleges have become a target not only for legitimate redress of ills, but sometimes, as the "Declaration of Campus Unrest" of the American Council on Education has indicated, for "a softening-up exercise for assault on the wider society."

To select a speech or two from the scores that have been given recently on student protests and administrative response to unrest is both difficult and arbitrary. The address by Malcolm Moos, reprinted below, seems, however, to be deserving of remembrance. Delivered at the annual convention of the American Newspaper Publishers Association in New York City on April 24, 1969, it

[5] Address delivered at the annual convention of the American Newspaper Publishers Association, New York City, April 24, 1969. Text furnished by Dr. Moos, with permission for this reprint.

[6] For biographical note, see Appendix.

presents a prudent balance among several essentials: sympathetic concern for reasonable student demands, administrative recognition of the need "to re-create the academic community," admission that the ills of the colleges and universities are reflections of a wider social malaise, and acknowledgment of society's need for an educational integrity that will help insure national survival.

Dr. Moos is the president of the University of Minnesota. A former professor of political science at Johns Hopkins University and a presidential adviser to the late Dwight D. Eisenhower, he is mentioned often as the speechwriter who had an important hand in the preparation of President Eisenhower's farewell address on the "military-industrial complex." As late as April 1969, *Newsweek* reported on Dr. Moos' role in shaping that address during the period 1958-1961. The current debate on the ABM system has given new thrust to the arguments set forth in the speech.

In a testy speech sometime after he otherwise disgraced himself by his emotional assaults on evolution during the celebrated Scopes trial or "Monkey Case," William Jennings Bryan observed: "The wise man is not the man who takes his children to the zoo on Sundays to look at the apes to show them how far we have come. No, the wise man," he said, "is the one who from time to time casts his eyes upward toward the heavens to remind himself how far he has yet to go."

Each of us, as we contemplate the brink of confusion, that surrounds the campus, can no longer doubt that this is a moment of national peril for higher education. Unless the next thirty years are to mark the dark age of the century, unless we are to see dreams strangled at birth, unless the ivory tower is to become a dark tower, unless we are to face unwelcome alternatives, one matter is altogether clear: the war between society and our children cannot continue.

American history, of course, abounds with disruption of many kinds, even though young people were thought to be relatively stable. But in part, that stability was myth, often masking deep schisms between youth and society. Certainly colleges and universities of the nineteenth century had their share of disruptive events. Lewis Feuer in his excellent book *The Conflict of Generations* reports that "Harvard students in the 1820's used to torment tutors by throwing cups, knives and biscuits at them during breakfast, and hurling pennies at the feet of professors leading them in prayer." By the late 1800's the University of California at Berkeley was also the center of similar student madcap behavior and misbehavior. One student raiding party swung a ladder back and forth against the window of the president's house, chanting obscene songs and breaking everything within that was breakable. When the president capitulated and resigned, not only the students but many of the faculty as well as regents rejoiced in his downfall. Today there is a startling catalog of campuses that have joined the University of California and Harvard in having serious problems with student disruptions.

Our own study shows that between September 1967 and June 1968 there were 250 campus disturbances and disruptions serious enough to attract notice by the nation's press, television, and radio media. As an historian, I thought it might be of some comparative interest to jump back thirty-two years to another period when some feared the nation might be breaking in two over the industrial sit-down strikes. In a comparable time span, September 1937 to June 1938, there were forty-five sit-down strikes. Early this year, in February alone there were varying degrees of incidents on fifty-five campuses.

Clearly in our race with time to cope with baffling problems the relationship of the universities to the press is central if the ivory tower is not to become a burning tower.

A very wise and skilled journalist and a member of Parliament, William Deeds, once made the very pithy comment that "news is something somebody doesn't want you to print." He also goes on to say that "the relations between the politician and newspapers are founded not on sympathy but antipathy. Both to some extent are rivals for influence over the public mind and they take good care that neither should achieve a monopoly of it." It is here he insists altogether correctly "where the great value of this relationship

lies, because in countries where newspapers and politicians
are in the same camp, freedom is threatened."

Universities, of course, are not politicians but the analogy
is relevant because universities do have a tremendous stake
in influencing the public mind. Yet our relationship with
the press cannot and must not be that of the sympathetic
partner, because the press must insist that no institutions of
our society achieve a monopoly of the public mind. Both
irresponsible and responsible stories in the press often en-
rage university administrators as well as faculty, but there
can be no shield from the slings and the arrows, no respite
from a world that cries aloud for remonstrance, resistance,
and remedies. For there can be no sanctuary from the bois-
terous thrusts of a probing press; universities can be wrong
and thumpingly so, and the more influential institutions become, the greater the menace to the public good where the
university has erred.

Any evaluation of embattled administrators attempting
to calm today's campus disorders must keep these factors
clearly in mind. First, universities operate in a quasi-legal
situation. The traditional codes of conduct are simply in-
adequate to deal with violence or serious disruption. It is
one matter to have rules governing hours or directed toward
keeping boys out of girls' dormitories, strictly another when
it comes to dealing with firearms, terrorism and the nonstudent interloper. Universities—and properly so in my judgment—do not believe that the long arm of the Federal Government should discipline the individual campus. Yet we are
confronted with two contradictory choices—one demonstrating that we can achieve order without depending upon
the police power of Federal or state authority—or the other
surely distasteful option of tightly structured national codes
setting up penalties with the backing of law.

A second nightmare for the university administrators is
what might be called the time scenario. Universities never
have been organized to accomplish objectives as of yesterday.
The academic community, in short, is just not tooled up to

move quickly. Structurally or temperamentally it is not set up to move speedily.

Ironically it is exactly a century since the appearance of Matthew Arnold's celebrated *Culture and Anarchy*, which raised the very questions that bedevil us today: should one appease the activist by responding immediately to demands or should one reach some general definition of what would be preferable before lurching into action. Arnold's conclusion, of course, is against accommodation to pressing demands of the activists. "We must decline to lend a hand to their operations," he writes, "until we for our own part at least, have grown a little clearer about the nature of the real good and have arrived nearer to a condition of mind out of which really fruitful and solid operations may spring."

But demands for black physics, white physics, black departments, black separatism, equal representation of students on faculty senates, paradoxical as they may appear to the academic community, are simply not going to await the traditional amiable pace of academic debate for solutions. The demands have escalated to the level of militancy of industrial strife as universities hasten to build negotiating and bargaining instruments to bring peace to the campus.

Many of the underlying causes of campus unsettlement are well known—the changing racial texture of society—the fact that suddenly half the population is under twenty-six, and a host of others. One of the most important changes is the emergence of the United States into a position of world leadership in a world in which modern weapons can quickly erase all life from our planet. Some young people say that we have become international policemen, constables without conscience. The distrust of old international methods has unleashed forces among our youth never before seen on the American campus. Searching for new answers in a society they despair of as dishonest, many students have embraced methods including both symbolic and mob violence.

Still other forces creating campus unrest are at work, one of the most important of which is the longevity of youth.

Essentially we have allowed the period of youth to be functionless in terms of engagement with society and the university, and that is what we're up against. Youth wants to participate in the world community, and passionately so, as recent events dramatically document. We saw this desire lash out in the McCarthy campaign as traditions were tilted and toppled in 1968. Everywhere some students desire to engage actively and continuously with the university community. We can almost smell the fumes of controversy and frustration arising out of the remark of a very attractive and bright young girl I met in England at the University of Sussex who railed at me: "Yes—we're angry—we're angry because we have time to be angry!" The paradox is that we support a functionless period for youth at the very time when we are considering lowering the voting age to eighteen and sending many young people to wars abroad.

So what we have is years of being an adult youth. And during this period—and increasingly so as a college education is becoming universal—the main relationship of youth is with his college or university. But colleges and universities are not families, and they cannot function as parents.

Yet with it all, the university must be their community. There must be some recognition of their status as responsible collegiate citizens, and means provided for informed participation in the tasks of building their community.

What we are dealing with is the problem of how communities establish the legitimacy of their laws, and the authenticity of their procedures for self-government. This requires, I believe, a community in which all members, all "citizens" are secure in the knowledge that they share in the "ownership" of their community. It requires a community willing and able to undertake the education of its new members, students, faculty, and administrators alike in both the rights and responsibilities of their citizenship. It requires a community able to clarify the necessity and justice of its rules as protections for common aspirations and securities for the rights of individuals. It requires a community in which the participation of student citizens in the processes of government should be viewed as a natural and legitimate goal. And it requires most of all a community ready, willing, and able to demonstrate that it can support by common consent, or support by discipline when merited, the quality of life essential to learning. We should make no mistake about this. We must govern ourselves, or others will assume this task for us. We must have faculties who are citizens of their community as well as expositors of a discipline. We must have students who join in these processes of self-government.

What is most important for the future well-being of our communities, however we accomplish it, is that we learn to listen to what young people are saying. When we do listen, we discover quickly that our youth are at war with hypocrisy —that this is, in fact, an honest generation.

No element of society is blameless when we search out the causes of campus disorder. Universities have been slow and unresponsive in many areas in developing reforms—quick to study others, slow to study themselves. We fuel the destructive notion that disruption is the path to reform by moving under the threat of chaos and doing business as usual when tensions seem low. Of course we're all preoccupied with trying to get through the spring term. But what are we doing to bring our educational program into tune with the necessities and aspirations of our students? And what are we doing to help them feel competent to deal with the world they inhabit today, and the changed world they will inhabit a decade or two from now? Do we imagine that the anxieties of our students about this world are not justified and that their search for better answers than the past has provided is not a search which should compel all of us?

Both universities and society generally must take note that subtle but profound changes are noticeable among not only the young militants but throughout the student body. Du Pont and other large corporations are noticing that recent graduates are not motivated by the same reward structure as the previous generation, and the Institute of the

Future at Wesleyan University, of which I am a director, is engaged in a fascinating study of this trend. Only yesterday the president of one of the world's largest banks noted in a lecture at the University of Minnesota that his brightest young staffer in his late twenties turned down a handsome raise, but asked for an assignment with the Urban Coalition —a fulfilled request that has made his work at the bank soar to even higher levels of achievement. In their quest for identity and purpose, many students reject authoritarianism. I recall that when the University of Minnesota took sophomore girls off hours some years ago we wrote to all parents asking them to indicate if they preferred to keep their daughters under university supervision. Only a few did. Most could not practice authoritarianism by requesting supervision even though they demanded that we practice administrative authoritarianism.

Administrators, tight against the barricades, of course, cannot blink the fact that we are confronted with a highly contradictory situation. Some of these students are exhausting, raucous rebels. They demand love from the very society they are smiting. They also demand to be rejected. Moreover, they insist upon playing both within and outside the old rules at the same time, depending, of course, on what is convenient at the moment.

We must recognize that not all students are alike, and that, in their search, they do not necessarily become a monolithic mass. Back in his days as a teacher of communication, S. I. Hayakawa pointed out that cow 1 is not the same as cow 2. It now seems equally clear that demonstrator 1 is not the same as demonstrator 2 either—and we need to recognize students as being different in goals, methods and attitudes. There simply is not a large group of revolutionary students on our campuses, but it is time we accept the fact that the lion's share of the student body wants major changes. If we are not flexible in the face of these requests for change, we run the risk of radicalizing our moderate students. Some students simply cannot accept the ambivalence of intellectual search. They are searching and grasping for something they can believe in.

Any overview of life on the campus ought to take note of the fact that psychiatric referrals are noticeably higher at some institutions—50 per cent higher at one institution—200 per cent at another.

Amidst the welter of contradictions that characterize student life and the terrific strains now on the university, what really are the options if we are to muddle through the crisis? We must begin, I believe, by demonstrating more constitutional ingenuity, strengthening faculty governmental institutions, and defining the student's role in the university's governance. We need to re-create the academic community— a most difficult feat because we have not really been inhabiting the academic community since in some ways it has ceased to exist. It is a formless jumble of disciplines that resemble guilds—a circumstance conducive to the development of systems of education rather than campus community. Strengthening faculty government can help offset this tendency by building more cross-structures, but this in turn requires that we gain the loyalty and confidence of the junior faculty—some of whom have been major factors in student disruption.

Strengthening the student's role in governance can also help. For the student thrust toward academic reform has, on the whole, been highly beneficial, and in many institutions today, students are making major contributions to institutional change. It is essential that the American press describe these contributions as fully as they often describe a disruptive event.

Finally this need for discovering some source of unity in our university community is so apparent that it leads me to the most critical change of all which must take place. I am persuaded, the more so after less than two years on the bridge of one of our large public universities, that university presidents must play a stronger role in the future of their institutions. I arrive at this position somewhat reluctantly. But you will recall the bullock, who, being pursued by a ferocious tiger in India shouted to a monkey: "Do you think I can climb this tree?" "Brother, it's no longer a matter of opinion. You've got to climb this tree."

There are no alternatives. The president must represent the university community in a new way, and this is a change that is certain to shake the bones and traditions of many academic communities.

In part this new necessity is thrust upon the president by the very magnitude of the interactions which occur in the modern world of learning. The sprawling bureaucracy of learning has fueled the knowledge explosion of the twentieth century, but it has led to a plaintive quest from students, from society, and from many faculty members as well for some point of contact with the whole life of an institution. How does a university speak? If it is to be a community, not only must it speak through the cacophony of a thousand academic voices in a hundred disciplines and professions, but also it must speak frequently and clearly as a unity, an idea and an ideal of the republic of learning. As valuable and essential as it is for the quiet murmur of inquiry, disputation, assertion, debate and intellectual friction to continue, it is also essential that the student talk to and hear from his university; that the citizen talk to and hear from his university; that all who seek some entry into the center find that a center exists. There is no rest and little chance of comfort for the president who takes his position as the symbolic center of a great diversity, but there is no turning back from the necessity that he take this position. Where the action is, there he must be.

The enlargement of the presidential role needs understanding by faculty, students, and trustees, all of whom share equally in the necessary search for a symbolic center to their community. The president is accountable, and in the life of the university it is proper that his accounting be made in the forums provided in his community. But it is also proper that an appropriate range of decision be attached to his office so that he may account for more than his diligence in mediating disputes, arranging parking and scrounging for funds. This is not to say that presidents should usurp power now assumed to be vested in the faculties, or trample thumpingly on the hopes and aspirations of students seeking a more muscular claim to their own corridors of power. It does not mean a concept that ascribes to the president, and to him alone, the mastery over events, the making of policy, or the administration of all acts of governance. But it does mean that delegation of a significant role for the president in the life of his community needs to be made; that he too should have some decisive piece of the action on the matters that count most in the life of his institution.

It would be easy to detail some possible areas of delegation in matters of university governance having to do with physical facilities, appellate procedure on conduct, fiscal analysis and the like. Indeed, in a variety of awkward ways, such delegations are commonplace. But let me turn to a more hazardous thought. The heart of a university is its community of scholars, and I would hope to see the day when this community develops a life style which includes students as fully participating members. Let me emphasize the words *fully participating,* for tokenism and condescension are quickly recognized for what they are by students. In this respect, an especially encouraging development at my own university has been the decision to include significant numbers of students as full members of the University Senate. This step is indicative of the growing role of students in the decision-making councils of the University.

Administrators too, must share fully in the new community. Today they participate either not at all, or only awkwardly in its invigoration. As a very modest proposal, it might be interesting to permit presidents to make a few academic appointments to leaven life on the campus. The number should be small; accountability should be strict; the price of foolishness would inevitably be more swift and severe than that visited upon a department trapped in some indiscretion.

But departments do become imbalanced and occasionally wither within to the point where there are no visible wraiths. But even more importantly, as universities move into and work with the world of the twentieth century, there are men who could enliven their communities, whose credentials fit no particular academic cage, but whose presence and participation would energize the intellectual climate. We have been greatly successful in recent years in nourishing the flow of academicians into the arenas of industry, commerce, and government. We have been diffident in our approach to the possibilities of a reverse flow. It would, I submit, be a plausible experiment for one or two foundations to undertake to fund four presidential chairs at each of our leading dozen universities. And it would be an experiment designed to identify the president, not merely as the voice of his community, but as a participant in its most fundamental aspirations. If he is to serve that which is in the transcendent interest of his community, he needs to become a full participant in its central life.

Admittedly the stakes in such a move are high, for if he fails, like Charles I, he must lose his head.

But the stakes are high for all of us. For society, if universities do not move vigorously in relation to the explosive problems of the world which surrounds them; for universities, if they do not bring students into full participation in the life of their community; for presidents, if they do not find, make visible, and move into the center of that community.

This problem cannot be dissolved or deflected by aimless debate or by taking refuge in the university's perversity to swift change.

Let me in closing turn for a moment to the part the press might play in examining the drama of campus disorder and change. I believe the press nationally, and the public as well, are fully aware of the fateful implications of the struggle now in process. In a nation committed to the faith that education can free men, it remains to be demonstrated that men can freely live at peace with one another and freely build just and fulfilling communities. The troubles of the campus are, in microcosm, the troubles of our entire society; the answers found by the campus will mirror inevitably either the flowering or the degradation of our entire society. The drama of campuses seeking the integrity and peace of true human communities deserves, therefore, both close and informed attention. Attention should be paid to the large number of decent men and women, faculty and students alike, who are seeking to find the sources and forms of community—to the problems they face, to their fumbling efforts at discovery, to their mistakes, and to what I believe will be their eventual success. The garish and absurd elements of this struggle and the demolition experts—both student and nonstudent—will not escape attention; they should not and must not obscure the story of search, trial, error, and social invention in which the form of all our futures may be determined.

IT IS TIME TO REASSESS OUR
NATIONAL PRIORITIES [7]

SHIRLEY CHISHOLM [8]

"Apparently all they know here in Washington about Brooklyn is that a tree grows there. I can think of no other reason for assigning me to the House Agriculture Committee." Those well-chosen words prefaced the statement by Shirley Chisholm in which she questioned the "petrified, sanctified system of seniority" which denied her her first and second choices for committee assignments in January 1969 in the United States House of Representatives. She found it hard "to imagine an assignment" that was less relevant to her background and to the needs of her constituency. Subsequently she was reassigned to the Committee on Veterans Affairs. Writing in the New York *Times Magazine,* Susan Brownmiller called the Chisholm balk "the most vivid sign of life in the Ninety-first Congress."

Mrs. Chisholm is an effective speaker and a skilled debater. Member of the debating society at Brooklyn College, holder of a master's degree, former teacher and educational consultant, Mrs. Chisholm served for four years (1965-1968) in the New York State Assembly. In 1968 she entered the race for Representative in Congress from the Twelfth District in Brooklyn. She won handily.

In 1969 two maiden speeches commanded wide attention. In late April, in the British House of Commons, twenty-one-year-old Bernadette Devlin, representing a Catholic constituency in Northern Ireland, pleaded eloquently for an end to the head smashing in Protestant-controlled Ulster. The other noteworthy maiden speech was given on March 26, 1969, before the United States House of Representatives. The speaker was Mrs. Shirley Chisholm. And her message was plain, forthright, and fearless. She announced boldly that

> I intend to vote No on every money bill that comes to the floor of this House that provides any funds for the Department of Defense. Any bill whatsoever, until the time comes when our values and priorities have been turned right side

[7] Address delivered before the United States House of Representatives, Washington, D.C., March 26, 1969. Text furnished by Shirley Downs, legislative assistant to Representative Chisholm, with permission for this reprint.

[8] For biographical note, see Appendix.

up again, until the monstrous waste and the shocking profits in the defense budget have been eliminated and our country starts to use its strength, its tremendous resources, for people and peace, not for profits and war.

The address bore out one of her claims: "I have a way of talking that does something to people."

On the same day President Nixon announced he had decided the United States will not be safe unless we start to build a defense system against missiles, the Head Start program in the District of Columbia was cut back for the lack of money.

As a teacher, and as a woman, I do not think I will ever understand what kind of values can be involved in spending $9 billion—and more, I am sure—on elaborate, unnecessary and impractical weapons when several thousand disadvantaged children in the nation's capital get nothing.

When the new Administration took office, I was one of the many Americans who hoped it would mean that our country would benefit from the fresh perspectives, the new ideas, the different priorities of a leader who had no part in its mistakes of the past. Mr. Nixon had said things like this: "If our cities are to be livable for the next generation, we can delay no longer in launching new approaches to the problems that beset them and to the tensions that tear them apart." And he said, "When you cut expenditures for education, what you are doing is shortchanging the American future."

But frankly, I have never cared too much what people say. What I am interested in is what they do. We have waited to see what the new Administration is going to do. The pattern now is becoming clear.

Apparently launching those new programs can be delayed for a while, after all. It seems we have to get some missiles launched first.

Recently the new Secretary of Commerce spelled it out. The Secretary, Mr. Stans, told a reporter that the new Administration is "pretty well agreed it must take time out from major social objectives" until it can stop inflation.

The new Secretary of Health, Education, and Welfare, Robert Finch, came to the Hill to tell the House Education and Labor Committee that he thinks we should spend more on education, particularly in city schools. But, he said, unfortunately we can't "afford" to, until we have reached some kind of honorable solution to the Vietnam war. I was glad to read that the distinguished Member from Oregon, Mrs. Green, asked Mr. Finch this: "With the crisis we have in education, and the crisis in our cities, can we wait to settle the war? Shouldn't it be the other way around? Unless we can meet the crisis in education, we really can't afford the war."

Secretary of Defense Melvin Laird came to Capitol Hill, too. His mission was to sell the antiballistic missile insanity to the Senate. He was asked what the new Administration is doing about the war. To hear him, one would have thought it was 1968, that the former Secretary of State was defending the former policies, that nothing had ever happened—a President had never decided not to run because he knew the nation would reject him, in despair over this tragic war we have blundered into. Mr. Laird talked of being prepared to spend at least two more years in Vietnam.

Two more years, two more years of hunger for Americans, of death for our best young men, of children here at home suffering the lifelong handicap of not having a good education when they are young. Two more years of high taxes, collected to feed the cancerous growth of a Defense Department budget that now consumes two thirds of our Federal income.

Two more years of too little being done to fight our greatest enemies—poverty, prejudice and neglect—here in our own country. Two more years of fantastic waste in the Defense Department and of penny-pinching on social programs. Our country cannot survive two more years, or four, of these kinds of policies. It must stop—this year—now.

Now I am not a pacifist. I am, deeply, unalterably, opposed to this war in Vietnam. Apart from all the other considerations, and they are many, the main fact is that we cannot squander there the lives, the money, the energy that we need desperately here, in our cities, in our schools.

I wonder whether we cannot reverse our whole approach to spending. For years, we have given the military, the defense industry, a blank check. New weapons systems are dreamed up, billions are spent, and many times they are found to be impractical, inefficient, unsatisfactory, even worthless. What do we do then? We spend more money on them. But with social programs, what do we do? Take the Job Corps. Its failures have been mercilessly exposed and criticized. If it had been a military research and development project, they would have been covered up or explained away, and Congress would have been ready to pour more billions after those that had been wasted on it.

The case of Pride, Inc., is interesting. This vigorous, successful black organization, here in Washington, conceived and built by young inner-city men, has been ruthlessly attacked by its enemies in the Government, in this Congress. At least six auditors from the General Accounting Office were put to work investigating Pride. They worked seven months and spent more than $100,000. They uncovered a fraud. It was something less than $2,100. Meanwhile millions of dollars—billions of dollars, in fact—were being spent by the Department of Defense, and how many auditors and investigators were checking into their negotiated contracts? Five.

We Americans have come to feel that it is our mission to make the world free. We believe that we are the good guys, everywhere, in Vietnam, in Latin America, wherever we go. We believe we are the good guys at home, too. When the Kerner Commission told white America what black America has always known, that prejudice and hatred built the nation's slums, maintains them and profits by them, white America would not believe it. But it is true. Unless we start to fight, and defeat, the enemies of poverty and racism in our own country and make our talk of equality and opportunity ring true, we are exposed as hypocrites in the eyes of the world when we talk about making other people free.

I am deeply disappointed at the clear evidence that the number one priority of the new Administration is to buy more and more and more weapons of war, to return to the era of the Cold War, to ignore the war we must fight here—the war that is not optional. There is only one way, I believe, to turn these policies around. The Congress can respond to the mandate that the American people have clearly expressed. They have said, "End this war. Stop the waste. Stop the killing. Do something for our own people first." We must find the money to "launch the new approaches," as Mr. Nixon said. We must force the Administration to rethink its distorted, unreal scale of priorities. Our children, our jobless men, our deprived, rejected and starving fellow citizens must come first.

For this reason, I intend to vote No on every money bill that comes to the floor of this House that provides any funds for the Department of Defense. Any bill whatsoever, until the time comes when our values and priorities have been turned right side up again, until the monstrous waste and the shocking profits in the defense budget have been eliminated and our country starts to use its strength, its tremendous resources, for people and peace, not for profits and war.

It was Calvin Coolidge, I believe, who made the comment that "the Business of America is Business." We are now spending $80 billion a year on defense—that is two thirds of every tax dollar. At this time, gentlemen, the business of America is War and it is time for a change.

INTERNATIONAL PERSPECTIVES

CHINA POLICY FOR THE SEVENTIES [1]

EDWARD M. KENNEDY [2]

Edward M. Kennedy of Massachusetts is one of the most skill-ful young politicians on the American scene. At thirty-seven, he displays a political astuteness and sophistication ordinarily asso-ciated only with the long-time veterans in the House of Repre-sentatives and the Senate. As Senate majority whip—a job which requires several hours daily on the floor—he is in a favored position, indeed, to sharpen his already acute talents for dealing with fellow Senators and for rounding up votes.

By virtue of his position as assistant majority leader, Mr. Kennedy is closely associated with Senator Mike Mansfield, a man of great influence in the nation. Shortly after Kennedy gave the address reprinted below, Mansfield asked that it be printed in the *Congressional Record* along with excerpts from his statement "The Pacific Perspective." Additionally, he remarked that Kennedy had made a contribution "in opening up the question of China"—since that country cannot be "obliterated by trying to make believe that it does not exist; because it does exist. . . . It is the great power on the Asian continent."

Coaches of debate in schools and colleges can bring to mind memories of forensic meets on the China question dating back many years. The bulk of the arguments used then are still perti-nent. Moreover, they have taken on added urgency because of China's nuclear potential, our proposed antiballistic missile system, which apparently is prompted in large part by fear of possible Chinese aggression, and our tarnished image in the Far East re-sulting from the Vietnam war. If we may believe the pronounce-ments of the Chinese leaders, as we doubtless should, the hard-line revolutionary program will go on, both in China and abroad. Against this sort of backdrop, Mr. Kennedy projected his argu-ment for a new China policy in a speech to the National Com-

[1] Speech delivered to the National Committee on United States-China Rela-tions, New York City, March 20, 1969. Text furnished by Senator Kennedy, with permission for this reprint.

[2] For biographical note, see Appendix.

mittee on United States-China Relations in New York City, on
March 20, 1969.

He called essentially for an abandonment of the old policy
of isolation toward Communist China and the adoption of a program which, in reasonable time, would result in the admission of
China to the United Nations, the reestablishment of consular offices in China, and the eventual resumption of diplomatic relations.
"For twenty years," he said, "our China policy has been a war
policy. For far too long, we have carried our hostile measures of
political, diplomatic, and economic antagonism toward one of the
world's most important nations." He urged therefore that we "turn
away from our policy of war and pursue a policy of peace."

This conference is one of the most important public
sessions on China policy in recent years. That fact alone is
extremely significant. The time at which this conference is
being held is also significant. For if we ever hoped that the
Communist regime in China would disappear, our hope is
in ruins today, as thousands of Chinese soldiers engage Russian border troops in the continuing struggle by two powerful
nations for domination of the world Communist movement.

Thousands of American soldiers are dying in Vietnam in
a land war in Asia whose purpose, we are told, is the containment of Peking. Demonstrations against American bases
in Japan and Okinawa—bases built in part to contain China
—shake the foundation of Japan. The shadow of Peking
hangs dark over the discussions in Paris and over virtually
every conference we attend on arms control. The success of
the Nuclear Nonproliferation Treaty, on which the ink is
hardly dry, depends in large part on the participation of
China.

If we ever hoped that somehow our relations with China
could be stabilized at a point of rigid hostility without domestic sacrifice, our hope was dashed when we were told
last week by our Government that we must now spend
$7 billion as a down payment to protect our missiles and our
nation from nuclear attack by China.

It is for these reasons that I consider this conference, and
what can come from it, so important to the foreign policy

of our nation. It is imperative that the issues you have discussed for so long become part of the national agenda of the United States. For almost twenty years, the United States has pursued the same unyielding policy of military containment and diplomatic isolation toward Communist China. However valid that policy may have seemed for the Cold War of the fifties, it is demonstrably false in the sixties, and must not be carried into the seventies.

Every new Administration has a new opportunity to rectify the errors of the past. Each such opportunity consists in large part of the precious gift of time—time in which the good intentions of the Government are presumed; time in which the normal conflicts of politics are suspended; time in which the new Government has a chance to show it is not tied to the policies of its predecessor.

If the new Administration allows this time to pass without new initiatives; if it allows inherited policies to rush unimpeded along their course, it will have wasted this opportunity. It will have compromised the promises it made to the American people, and worst of all, it will have disappointed the hopes and expectations of the world.

This is especially true in Vietnam. There is growing impatience with the continuing loss of American lives and the seeming frustration of our hopes for the reduction of violence and for the reduction of the American commitment. The advent of a new Administration affords a moment of hope for millions of Americans and Vietnamese. It is a moment that will not long be with us.

The same opportunity exists for our policies throughout Asia. That is why it is all the more important that you who have been involved in the formulation and evaluation of those policies, both in private life and public service, meet here at this time to chart your recommendations.

For twenty years, our China policy has been a war policy. For far too long, we have carried out hostile measures of political, diplomatic, and economic antagonism toward one of the world's most important nations.

Now we must turn away from our policy of war and pursue a policy of peace. We must seek a new policy, not because of any supposed weakness in our present position or because we are soft on China, but because it is in our own national interest and the interest of all nations. By its sheer size and population, China deserves a major place in the world. As a nuclear power and a nation of 750 million citizens—likely to exceed one billion by the 1980's—China demands a voice in world efforts to deal with arms control and population control, with Asian security and international economic development, with all the great issues of our time.

Yet sixteen years after the end of the Korean War, we do not trade with China. We have no scientific or cultural exchanges. We oppose the representation of China in the United Nations. We refuse to give any sort of diplomatic recognition to the Communist regime on the mainland, and continue to recognize the Nationalist regime of Chiang Kai-shek on Taiwan as the government of all China. Instead of developing ways to coexist with China in peace, we assume China will attack us as soon as she can, and we prepare to spend billions to meet that threat.

By some cruel paradox, an entire generation of young Americans and young Chinese have grown to maturity with their countries in a state of suspended war toward one another. Tragically, the world's oldest civilization and the world's most modern civilization, the world's most populous nation and the world's richest and most powerful nation, glare at each other across the abyss of nuclear war.

The division between us goes back to American support of the Chinese Nationalist regime during World War II, and to the immediate postwar struggle between the Communists and the Nationalists. In the beginning, our policy was uncertain. The Communists gained power over the mainland in 1949. Between then and the outbreak of the Korean War in 1950, the United States seemed to be preparing to accept the fact of the Chinese Revolution. After the retreat of the Nationalists to Taiwan, our Government refused to go to their aid and refused to place the American Seventh Fleet in the Taiwan Strait to prevent a Communist take-over of the island. To do so, we said, would be to intervene in the domestic civil war between the Communists and the Nationalists.

This policy was fully debated by the Congress and the public. Although we deplored the Communist rise to power, we recognized we could do nothing to change it. We anticipated that we would soon adjust to the new Asian reality by establishing relations with the Communist regime.

This situation changed overnight on June 25, 1950, when North Korea attacked South Korea. Fearing that the attack foreshadowed a Communist offensive throughout Asia, the United States ordered the Seventh Fleet into the Taiwan Strait and sent large amounts of military aid to the weak Nationalist government on the island. To the Communists, the meaning was clear. We would use force to deny Taiwan to the new mainland government, even though both the Communists and the Nationalists agreed the island was Chinese.

Shortly thereafter, in response to the attempt of our forces to bring down the North Korean government by driving toward the Chinese border, China entered the Korean War. With hindsight, most experts agree that China's action in Korea was an essentially defensive response, launched to prevent the establishment of a hostile government on her border. At the time, however, the issue was far less clear. At the request of the United States, the United Nations formally branded China as an aggressor, a stigma that rankles Peking's leaders even today.

While we fought the Chinese in Korea, we carried out a series of political and economic actions against their country. We imposed a total embargo on all American trade with the mainland. We froze Peking's assets in the United States. We demanded that our allies limit their trade with China. We conducted espionage and sabotage operations against the mainland, and supported similar efforts by the Nationalists. We began to construct a chain of bases, encircling China with American military power, including nuclear weapons.

It is not my purpose here to question the merits of the actions we took while fighting China in Korea. We all remember the climate of those times and the great concern of our country with Chinese military actions. Today, however, sixteen years after the Korean armistice was signed, we have taken almost no significant steps to abandon our posture of war toward China and to develop relations of peace.

Let us look at our policy from the viewpoint of Peking: China's leaders see the United States supporting the Nationalists' pretense to be the government of the mainland. They see thousands of American military personnel on Taiwan. American warships guard the waters between the mainland and Taiwan. American nuclear bases and submarines ring the periphery of China. The United States supports Nationalist U-2 flights over the mainland, as well as Nationalist guerrilla raids and espionage. Hundreds of thousands of American soldiers are fighting in Vietnam to contain China. America applies constant diplomatic and political pressure to deny Peking a seat in the United Nations, to deny it diplomatic recognition by the nations of the world, and to deny it freedom of trade. We turn our nuclear warheads toward China. And now we prepare to build a vast ABM system to protect ourselves against China. In light of all these facts, what Chinese leader would dare to propose anything but the deepest hostility toward the United States?

With respect to the ABM question, I am strongly opposed for many reasons to the deployment of the Pentagon's system. For the purpose of the present discussion, however, one of its most significant drawbacks is that it is likely to be seen in Peking as a new military provocation by the United States. Our overwhelming nuclear arsenal already provides adequate deterrence against any temptation by Peking to engage in a first strike against the United States. From the

Chinese perspective, the only utility of an American ABM system is to defend the United States against whatever feeble response Peking could muster after an American first strike against China. Far from deterring aggression by China, therefore, deployment of the ABM system will simply add fuel to our warlike posture toward China. It will increase Chinese fears of American attack and will encourage China's leaders to embark on new steps in the development of their nuclear capability. Apart from the technical and other policy objections that exist against the ABM system, I believe it makes no sense from the standpoint of a rational Asia policy for America.

In large part, our continuing hostility toward China after the Korean War has rested on a hope that is now obviously forlorn, a hope that under a policy of military containment and political isolation the Communist regime on the mainland would be a passing phenomenon and would eventually be repudiated by the Chinese people. Few of us today have any serious doubt that communism is permanent for the foreseeable future on the mainland. There is no believable prospect that Chiang Kai-shek and the Nationalists will return to power there, however regrettable we may regard that fact.

Surely, in the entire history of American foreign policy, there has been no fiction more palpably absurd than our official position that Communist China does not exist. For twenty years, the Nationalists have controlled only the 2 million Chinese and 11 million Taiwanese on the Island of Taiwan, one hundred miles from the mainland of China. How long will we continue to insist that the rulers of Taiwan are also the rulers of the hundreds of millions of Chinese on the millions of square miles of the mainland? It is as though the island of Cuba were to claim sovereignty over the entire continent of North America.

The folly of our present policy of isolating China is matched by its futility. Almost all other nations have adjusted to the reality of China. For years, Peking has had extensive diplomatic, commercial and cultural relations with a number of the nations in the world, including many of our closest allies. Outside the United Nations, our policy of quarantine toward China has failed. To the extent that the Communist regime is isolated at all, it is isolated largely at China's own choosing, and not as a consequence of any effective American policy.

Our actions toward China have rested on the premise that the People's Republic is an illegitimate, evil and expansionist regime that must be contained until it collapses or at least begins to behave in conformity with American interests. Secretary of State Dulles was the foremost exponent of this moralistic view, carrying it to the extent that he even refused to shake hands with Chou En-lai at the Geneva Conference in 1954. That slight has not been forgotten.

The Communist regime was said to be illegitimate because, we claimed, it had been imposed on the supposedly unreceptive Chinese people by agents of the Soviet Union. Communist China, according to this view, was a mere Soviet satellite. One Assistant Secretary in the State Department called it a Soviet Manchukuo, suggesting that China's new leaders were no more independent than were the Chinese puppets whom Japan installed in Manchuria in the 1930's. This evaluation grossly exaggerated the extent to which Soviet aid was responsible for the Communist takeover of China, and the events of the past decade—amply confirmed by the intense hostility of the current border clashes—have shattered the myth of Soviet domination of China.

The Communist regime was said to be evil because of the great violence and deprivation of freedom that it inflicted on millions of people who opposed its rise to power. Obviously, we cannot condone the appalling cost, in human life and suffering, of the Chinese Revolution. Yet, in many other cases, we have recognized revolutionary regimes, especially when the period of revolutionary excess has passed. Even in the case of the Soviet Union, the United States waited only sixteen years to normalize relations with the revolutionary government.

Unfortunately, we have tended to focus exclusively on the costs of the Chinese revolution. We have ignored the historical conditions that evoked it and the social and economic gains it produced. We have ignored the fact that the Nationalists also engaged in repressive measures and deprivations of freedom, not only during their tenure on the mainland, but also on Taiwan. We have created a false image of a struggle between "Free China" and "Red China," between good and evil. Given our current perspective and the greater understanding of revolutionary change that has come with time, we can now afford a more dispassionate and accurate review of the Chinese Revolution.

Finally, there is the charge that the Communist regime is an expansionist power. At bottom, it is this view that has given rise to our containment policy in Asia, with the enormous sacrifices it has entailed. The charge that the Communist regime is expansionist has meant different things at different times. On occasion, American spokesmen have conjured up the image of a "Golden Horde" or "Yellow Peril" that would swoop down over Asia. Today, most leaders in Washington employ more responsible rhetoric, and it is the Russians who perpetuate this image of China.

Virtually no experts on China expect Peking to commit aggression, in the conventional sense of forcibly occupying the territory of another country—as the Soviet Union recently occupied Czechoslovakia. Such action is in accord with neither past Chinese actions nor present Chinese capabilities. Despite their ideological bombast, the Chinese Communists have in fact been extremely cautious about risking military involvement since the Korean War. The Quemoy crises of the 1950's and the 1962 clash with India were carefully limited engagements. The struggle over Tibet is widely regarded as a reassertion of traditional Chinese jurisdiction over that remote area. China has not used force to protect the overseas Chinese in the disturbances in Burma, Malaysia, or Indonesia. Her navy and air force are small. She can neither transport her troops nor supply them across the long distances and difficult terrain of a prolonged war of aggression.

Obviously, our concern today is not so much the danger of direct Chinese aggression as the danger of indirect aggression, based on Chinese efforts to subvert existing governments and replace them with governments friendly to Peking. Yet, until Vietnam led to our massive involvement in Southeast Asia, Peking enjoyed only very limited success in its attempts to foster "wars of national liberation." Although China of course will claim to play a role wherever political instability occurs in Asia, Africa and even Latin America, its record of subversion is unimpressive. On the basis of the past, it is very likely that nations whose governments work for equality and social justice for their people will be able to overcome any threat of Chinese subversion.

Furthermore, we can expect that time will moderate China's revolutionary zeal. Experience with the Soviet Union and the Eastern European Communist nations suggests that the more fully China is brought into the world community, the greater will be the pressure to behave like a nation-state, rather than a revolutionary power.

Ironically, it is Communist China's former teacher, the Soviet Union, that is now determined to prevent any moderation of Chinese-American hostility. We cannot accept at face value the current Soviet image of China, for the Soviets have far different interests in Asia than we do. Although we must persist in our efforts to achieve wider agreement with Moscow, we must not allow the Russians to make continuing hostility toward Peking the price of future Soviet-American cooperation. Rather than retard our relations with Moscow, a Washington-Peking thaw might well provide the Soviet Union with a badly needed incentive to improve relations with us.

We must not, however, regard relations with Peking and Moscow as an either-or proposition. We must strive to improve relations with both. We must be alert, therefore, to any opportunity offered by the escalating hostility between China and the Soviet Union to ease our own tensions with those nations.

Both of us—Chinese and Americans alike—are prisoners of the passions of the past. What we need now, and in the decades ahead, is liberation from those passions. Given the history of our past relations with China, it is unrealistic to expect Peking to take the initiative. It is our obligation. We are the great and powerful nation, and we should not condition our approach on any favorable action or change of attitude by Peking. For us to begin a policy of peace would be a credit to our history and our place in the world today. To continue on our present path will lead only to further hostility, and the real possibility of mutual destruction.

Of course, we must not delude ourselves. Even if the United States moves toward an enlightened China policy, the foreseeable prospects for moderating Chinese-American tensions are not bright. It is said that there is no basis for hope so long as the current generation of Communist Chinese leaders remains in power. This may well be true. Yet, Peking's invitation last November to resume the Warsaw talks, although now withdrawn, suggests the possibility that China's policy may change more rapidly than outside observers can now anticipate.

We must remember, too, that the regime in Peking is not a monolith. As the upheavals of the Great Leap Forward and the Cultural Revolution have shown, China's leaders are divided by conflicting views and pressures for change. We must seek to influence such change in a favorable direction. We can do so by insuring that reasonable options for improved relations with the United States are always available to Peking's moderate or less extreme leaders.

The steps that we take should be taken soon. Even now, the deterioration of Chinese-Soviet relations in the wake of the recent border clashes may be stimulating at least some of the leaders in Peking to reevaluate their posture toward the United States and provide us with an extraordinary opportunity to break the bonds of distrust.

What can we do to hasten the next opportunity? Many of us here tonight are already on record as favoring a more positive stand. We must actively encourage China to adopt the change in attitude for which we now simply wait. We must act now to make clear to the Chinese and to the world that the responsibility for the present impasse no longer lies with us.

First, and most important, we should proclaim our willingness to adopt a new policy toward China—a policy of peace, not war, a policy that abandons the old slogans, embraces today's reality, and encourages tomorrow's possibility. We should make clear that we regard China as a legitimate power in control of the mainland, entitled to full participation as an equal member of the world community and to a decent regard for its own security. The policy I advocate will in no way impede our ability to respond firmly and effectively to any possibility of attack by the Chinese. What it will do, however, is emphasize to China that our military posture is purely defensive, and that we stand ready at all times to work toward improvement in our relations.

Second, we should attempt to reconvene the Warsaw talks. At the time the talks were canceled, I wrote the Secretary of State, asking the Administration to make an urgent new attempt to establish the contact that we so nearly achieved at Warsaw, and to do so before the air of expectancy that hung over the talks is completely dissipated. If the talks are resumed, we should attempt to transform them into a more confidential and perhaps more significant dialogue. The parties might meet on an alternating basis in their respective embassies, or even in their respective countries, rather than in a palace of the Polish Government. Whether or not the talks are resumed, more informal official and semiofficial conversations with China's leaders should be offered.

Third, we should unilaterally do away with restrictions on travel and nonstrategic trade. We should do all we can to promote exchanges of people and ideas, through scientific and cultural programs and access by news media representatives. In trade, we should place China on the same footing as the Soviet Union and the Communist nations of Eastern Europe. We should offer to send trade delegations and even a resident trade mission to China, and to receive Chinese trade delegations and a Chinese trade mission in this country. Finally, we should welcome closer contacts between China and the rest of the world, rather than continue to exert pressure on our friends to isolate the Peking regime.

Fourth, we should announce our willingness to reestablish the consular offices we maintained in the People's Republic during the earliest period of Communist rule, and we should welcome Chinese consular officials in the United States. Consular relations facilitate trade and other contacts. They frequently exist in the absence of diplomatic relations, and often pave the way for the establishment of such relations.

Fifth, we should strive to involve the Chinese in serious arms control talks. We should actively encourage them to begin to participate in international conferences, and we should seek out new opportunities to discuss Asian security and other problems.

Sixth, we should seek, at the earliest opportunity, to discuss with China's leaders the complex question of the establishment of full diplomatic relations. For the present, we should continue our diplomatic relations with the Nationalist regime on Taiwan and guarantee the people of that island against any forcible take-over by the mainland. To Peking, at this time, the question of diplomatic recognition seems to be unavoidably linked to the question of whether we will withdraw recognition from the Nationalists and the question of whether Taiwan is part of the territory of China. Both the Communists and the Nationalists claim Taiwan as part of China, but our own Government regards the status of the island as undefined, even though we maintain diplomatic relations with the Nationalists.

We have failed to agree on solutions involving other divided countries and peoples—as in Germany—and we cannot be confident of greater success in the matter of Taiwan. There are critical questions that simply cannot now be answered:

Will the minority regime of the Chinese Nationalists continue to control the island's Taiwanese population?

Will the Taiwanese majority eventually transform the island's government through the exercise of self-determination?

Will an accommodation be worked out between a future Taiwan Government and the Peking regime on the mainland?

To help elicit Peking's interest in negotiations, we should withdraw our token American military presence from Taiwan. This demilitarization of Taiwan could take place at no cost to our treaty commitments, or to the security of the island. Yet, it would help to make clear to Peking our desire for the Communists, the Nationalists, and the Taiwanese to reach a negotiated solution on the status of the island.

A dramatic step like unilateral recognition of Peking would probably be an empty gesture at this time. As the experience of France implies, unilateral recognition of Peking is not likely to be effective unless it is accompanied by the withdrawal of our existing recognition of the Nationalists. And, as the case of Great Britain suggests, Peking may insist on our recognition of the mainland's claim to Taiwan before allowing us to establish full ambassadorial relations. These problems will have to be negotiated, and we should move now to start the process.

Seventh, without waiting for resolution of the complex question of Taiwan, we should withdraw our opposition to Peking's entry into the United Nations as the representative of China, not only in the General Assembly, but also in the Security Council and other organs. The Security Council seat was granted to China in 1945 in recognition of a great people who had borne a major share of the burden in World War II, thereby making the United Nations possible. It was not a reward for the particular political group that happened to be running the country at the time.

In addition, we should work within the United Nations to attempt to assure representation for the people on Taiwan that will reflect the island's governmental status. It may be that the Chinese Nationalists can continue to enjoy a seat in the General Assembly. Or, if an independent republic of Taiwan emerges, it might be admitted into the United Nations as a new state. Possibly, if a political accommodation is reached between the Communist regime on the mainland and the government on Taiwan, the people of Taiwan might be represented in the United Nations as an autonomous unit of China, by analogy to the present status of Byelorussia and the Ukraine in the United Nations as autonomous provinces of the Soviet Union.

From its inception, the United Nations has displayed remarkable flexibility in adjusting to political realities. There are many possible solutions to the China problem in the United Nations. Without insisting on any one, we should move now to free the United Nations to undertake the long-delayed process of adjusting to the reality of the People's Republic of China, and we should clearly indicate to Peking our willingness to discuss these questions.

In dealing with the problems of diplomatic recognition and United Nations representation, I have placed primary emphasis on the need to initiate discussions with Peking in these areas. Since it is impossible to predict when or how the Chinese will respond to a change in American policy, we cannot maintain a hard and fast position on these questions. We cannot afford to close any options by endorsing detailed schemes at this time. What we can do, however, is act now on the broad range of initiatives I have mentioned, and make clear to Peking that our views are not rigid on even the most difficult issues that have divided us so bitterly in recent years.

We will have to be patient. Peking's initial reaction to serious initiatives on our part will probably be a blunt refusal. But, by laying the groundwork now for an improved relationship in the seventies and beyond, we will be offering the present and future leaders in Peking a clear and attractive alternative to the existing impasse in our relations.

Many outstanding authorities on China are here tonight. Perhaps I can sum up my central theme in terms that you may find appropriate. According to Chinese tradition, the model Confucian gentleman was taught that, whenever involved in a dispute, he should first examine his own behavior, ask himself whether he bears some responsibility for the dispute, and take the initiative to try to arrive at a harmonious settlement.

It may prove futile for us to follow this advice when dealing with Chinese who claim to reject many of China's great traditions. But we will never know unless we try. If nothing changes, we Americans will have to live with the consequences of arms and fear and war. We owe ourselves, we owe the future, a heavy obligation to try.

A LONG VIEW OF THE SHORT RUN [3]

WALTER B. WRISTON [4]

Speeches before international organizations often pose unusual challenges. Not uncommonly, there are cross-purposes of belief and feeling linked to national interests; there may be fears and anxieties about the policies—expressed or practiced—by the country which the speaker represents; suspicion may exist of the role of the world power in the community of smaller nations. The following speech is a deft blend of themes and methods designed to draw such an audience closely and warmly together.

In his address before the International Chamber of Commerce in Copenhagen, Denmark, on October 24, 1968, Walter B. Wriston, president of the First National City Bank of New York, viewed certain events, both in the United States and other countries, which currently hold the world in unremitting tension. In his talk, he touched subtly upon the alleged challenge, if not threat, of American technology and management to the European nations. Through it all he stressed the central idea that "we appear to be short of long views; we have become inept in sorting out the signs." Optimistically, however, he concluded that

> if we take the longer view of the short run, and balance the turbulent vocal strivings of a democracy against those systems which do not place the individual at the center, we will ask with Lincoln, the true American challenger, "Why should there not be a patient confidence in the ultimate justice of the people? Is there any better or equal hope in the world?"

America-watchers in Europe are naturally fascinated with the prospects of one candidate or another in our presidential election. So strong is the interest, Europeans greet even me as a political seer. The fact is, of course, I am only a banker and I cannot tell you who will be elected President

[3] Address delivered before the International Chamber of Commerce, Copenhagen, Denmark, October 24, 1968. Text furnished by Donald J. Colen, vice president, First National City Bank, New York, with permission for this reprint.

[4] For biographical note, see Appendix.

of the United States in the next three weeks. But I can tell you with confidence that the election will take place, which is no small assurance about the stability of democratic institutions in a world that is laced with riot and reaction. In short, America is not going to pot regardless of what you may read about the activities of our youth, or the well-publicized preoccupation of their parents with affluence.

In saying this, I do not mean to imply we do not have any problems on our side of the water. It is even fair to say all is not right with my country, or any other country anywhere. But what ails America ails the world—if that is the word. For everywhere man does not quite accept Søren Kierkegaard's suggestion that "life can only be understood backwards, but it must be lived forward."

The symptoms of chaos are all around us. It is not only the riots in Chicago, Paris, Tokyo, Prague and Peking; or blacks and whites massed against each other; or cries for law and order that make you wonder where justice went. What is even more disturbing is that the conflicting signs apparently are totally inconsistent and therefore appear to make little sense.

Hanoi applauded the rape of Prague, and Peking scorned it. Revolutionary students—in the West at least—march not to throw off political and economic oppression, but freely as the sons of affluence. Europe's left is violently anti-American, yet one of its own mainstays is my country's anticolonialism, which it often refuses to recognize. Our economies have never benefited so much from expanded foreign trade, but our governments concentrate on designing controls and obstructions to the free flow of men, money and ideas.

It may just be, however, that one key to our troubles lies in our interpretations. Much less a show of overbearing strength, the strangulation of Czechoslovakia's demonstration of a small measure of freedom was more likely a sign of weakness. What is taken for United States anti-Gaullism did not prevent the United States from supporting the French franc in its time of trouble. There are a multitude of other examples. What they all indicate is that we appear to be short of long views; we have become inept in sorting out the signs. In the next few minutes I should like to try to throw into perspective some of the events that have the world in their grip, and in the process, to say a kind word for the human race in general, and for that part of it which inhabits the Western world in particular.

Look first at our preoccupation with posterity. Futurism has become a serious undertaking. In England, France and the United States, expertly staffed and well-financed organizations are peering toward the year 2000 in search of certainty. One of the attractions, of course, is in the millennial nature of the year. Another reason we are so concerned with tomorrow, as many sociologists and historians tell us, is that in times of trouble, man has always wrapped himself protectively in the future, exchanging vague hopes for precise fears.

The development of new decision-making theories and mathematical techniques appears to impart a degree of predictive assurance that we have never known before. Now, with the perfection of advanced computers, it begins to look as though in the 2,500 years since Delphi we can measure our progress by the substitution of electrons for entrails.

The computer's seeming certainty and its way of neatly printing out in ordered rows what we have already instructed it to do give us false confidence that our extrapolations are errorproof. It is just this feeling of certainty which has produced too many speeches predicting that the end of the world will come tomorrow at 12:00 noon if this or that doesn't happen, and happen promptly. There have been too many pontifical pronouncements made about the world's events which have been reversed in tomorrow's headlines.

Some say that advances in the technology of mass communication make us better informed and less likely to be deceived. Better communications were devised to tie the world together more closely, and it may be so, but it also accentuates our differences and proliferates what Raymond Aron calls the "coefficients of uncertainty." We have too much data and not enough information. The very speed with which the news is communicated by printed media and especially television, within countries and around the world by satellite, produces nothing more definite to the untrained eye than a Jackson Pollock painting. News becomes an interminable stream mixing trivia with trends, and tends to defy interpretation. The current history of the world supplies an unlimited number of examples.

Certainly everyone in this room remembers the scholars, diplomats and common people who spoke confidently of the new détente between Russia and the West, and how the current management in the Kremlin had learned a little more about humanitarianism than the old Stalin regime. The same kind of talk was prevalent just before the bloody Hungarian revolution and reached almost a crescendo just a week before Prague.

From the lesson of events such as these, one of the fundamental axioms to remember is that the communications media, as well as history, record only what happened, and they record it imperfectly. They rarely specify the alternatives. The average or even the exceptional person today tends to think that President Kennedy won the presidency overwhelmingly. The facts, of course, are that he defeated Mr. Nixon by only about 119,000 votes out of the 69 million cast, and he did not even secure a majority of the votes cast. Similarly, how the voting ranged in the Politburo for the current Russian leaders will undoubtedly remain unknown for many years. But the chances are that it was no more overwhelming a demonstration of unanimity than what we see in our Western democracies.

And looking back even further, what unrecorded alternatives would have improved our ability to foresee the events of the last half century? In 1939, for example, it might have been possible to predict the breakup of colonial empires and the rise of Russia and the United States to positions of preeminent power. This was noted by many observers over a century ago. But who would have seen a Communist China of today's proportions, or the spread of the idea of development, or the balance of nuclear terror, or a return to the very ancient concept of guerrilla warfare as the determinant of nationalistic development in a world of atomic capabilities?

Nor, it seems to me, could anyone have been more far-seeing after World War II, especially in view of the incredible proliferation of technological developments. Even here the record is uncertain. The computer was only an integrating machine; the transistor that made the high speed computer possible was a long way downstream; television, the fuel cell, atomic physics—all of these developments and innumerable others were in some instances only speculations, in others still unthought of. Yet for all our inability to know all of the alternatives, or to draw the outlines of tomorrow with any certainty, we still look to technology to help us play God.

Currently, Servan-Schreiber's book *The American Challenge* is the subject of debate, conversation and intellectual stimulation. Like many books that cause a sensation, it influences those who actually have not read it even more than those who have, as *Das Kapital* attests so well. If I read Mr. Servan-Schreiber correctly, he says that the American challenge is the challenge of technology and the advanced management concepts that it spawns. But what I suggest to you today is that the American challenge he writes about with a good deal of insight is not the American challenge which in the long view is the most important to our friends in Europe or in the rest of the world.

The American challenge that has really changed, is changing and will continue to change the history of the world is the assumption that is bred into our bones, that the individual is of infinite worth, and therefore that individual human freedom is the most important political objective.

When this startling doctrine was launched in 1776, the group of colonies attempting to become the United States of America were so small, so weak, so remote and so insignificant that they were not to be taken seriously. But within decades, the American experience did, in fact, begin to spread across the seas, and it was Thomas Paine, the American pamphleteer of freedom, who wrote, "My country is the world." His words reached relatively few men, but in the last fifty years, the growth in the power of the United States has made this particular challenge one that compels the attention of the rest of the world.

Because of the sheer size and power of the United States, our domestic local conflicts and indiscretions become a source of worldwide concern as they are beamed to Europe in living color via the satellite. The old establishments of the world look with understandable displeasure upon a country that appears to have a continuing and permanent revolution. It is not a comfortable feeling for any power elite, whether governmental or industrial, to observe a society that is in a constant rapid rate of social change attempting to validate the proposition that all men are created equal. The explosion of knowledge, as evidenced by the almost 60 million people in my country who are involved in education as a primary occupation, and the marriage of the industrial manager with the intellectual are shifting the locus of our society at an astonishing rate.

Toynbee's statement that "civilization is a movement and not a condition, a voyage and not a harbor" does nothing to calm the nerves of those who embrace the concept of change intellectually, but fear it in their hearts. The export of this revolutionary doctrine of freedom is responsible for the fact that beside the picture of the local hero in the far corners of the world I have seen the picture of our President Abraham Lincoln, and I have listened to the South American patriot Bolivar being referred to as the George Washington of Latin America. You can walk down a Kennedy Gade virtually anywhere in the world and you will find statues of American Presidents in town parks and squares wherever the call of freedom is heard.

I was in Europe when President Eisenhower sent troops into Little Rock. That event spurred a wave of anti-American sentiment and the belief was expressed that my country had started down the road to fascism. It was immensely difficult to explain to my friends that rather than a show of totalitarianism, those troops were there to enforce the guarantees of individual rights contained in our Constitution. Nor is there much more understanding of the American challenge today.

Our democratic processes and the ways of our elections are still mysterious, and that mystery only hobbles efforts, even in America, to achieve the necessary perspective that I mentioned earlier. Consider the spectacle of our political conventions with the immaculate orderliness of the Republicans in Miami and the equally unreasoned bedlam of the Democrats in Chicago. Yet instead of being rigged, our national political conventions were expressions of the will of a majority of American voters.

Every one of the opinion surveys showed that a majority of registered Republicans favored Nixon and a majority of registered Democrats favored Humphrey. That the losers were articulate and able and had the active sympathy and support of the media does not change the fact. What is more, even though Europeans view the progress of black Americans as excruciatingly slow, no nation has ever made so concerted or concentrated an effort to better the position of a minority, as Gunnar Myrdal has pointed out.

We should understand with de Tocqueville that "the world is a strange theater. There are moments in it when the worst plays are those which succeed the best."

With a show of perspective, we should understand the true meaning of the London *Economist's* recent question, "What was Europe, Daddy?" And the *Economist* went on, in part:

The answer our grandchildren seem likeliest to get to that question is that it was the old-fashioned name for the geographical area where the Russian world and the American world happened to meet. Seldom has Europe seemed less effective than it does now. Four of its nation-states have just ganged up with their Russian

masters to suppress the libertarian desires of a fifth. The remainder
—a group whose population is as large as, and whose gross national
product is substantially greater than, those of the aggressors—have
stood helplessly by, not because the Americans told them to, but
because the Europeans had neither the unity, nor the means, nor
the will to do anything else.

If this is a harsh indictment, it is no less stringent than
the accusation that America and Russia have an agreement
to divide the world into spheres of interest and that Prague
occurred only because America connived in a hands-off policy. If we hurl epithets across the Atlantic it is only because
we all see different demons.

Look objectively for a moment at what has been called
the "Americanization of Europe," and I think there is no one
in this room who would not agree that what is really implied
is the equalization of society. It occurred only because there
is a direct correlation between productivity, education and
the diminution of political authority. With economic growth
has come an egalitarian trend that is political as well as economic. On the political side, we have witnessed a spread of
literacy, the extension of education and the proliferation of
freedom.

On the economic side, equalization induced by technological and organizational advances has brought a sharp
improvement in the upward mobility of the members of society. Man everywhere now scorns the notion that poverty is
a necessary school which leads to advancement. And from
these developments have come the fruits of the true American challenge; namely, a new democratic ideology—new to
many parts of the world—that the state belongs to the people.

All together, then, we can say that our ultimate need is to
bring a measure of perspective to our judgments—to apply
the lessons of history to the intense cross-purposes and currents of the present. We need to look at the demand for so-
called law and order against violence, and to understand
with Burke that "the use of force is but temporary. It may
subdue for a moment, but it does not remove the necessity

for subduing again: and a nation is not governed which is perpetually to be conquered."

How then will our nations be governed? Not surely as a perpetual search for heroic solutions, despite what youth tells us. Perhaps instead we ought to follow the lead of the scientists who, as they have pointed out, do not "leap from hilltop to hilltop, from triumph to triumph, or from discovery to discovery." They proceed from a process of exploration in which they sometimes learn to do better. This is what we ought to do in the affairs of men. This, too, is what some others of the young are also trying to tell us. They are saying, as Whitehead said, that the art of free society consists in the fearlessness of revision.

And so if we take the longer view of the short run, and balance the turbulent vocal strivings of a democracy against those systems which do not place the individual at the center, we will ask with Lincoln, the true American challenger, "Why should there not be a patient confidence in the ultimate justice of the people? Is there any better or equal hope in the world?"

A PACIFIC PERSPECTIVE [5]

MIKE MANSFIELD [6]

In an address on March 22, 1969, at the Ninth Annual West Side Community Conference in New York, former Senator Wayne Morse (Democrat) of Oregon remarked:

> In Asia, we have worked a "domino theory" in reverse. To defend the United States, we needed Pacific Islands like the Marianas put under our trusteeship; then to protect those islands, we needed Japan, Okinawa, Formosa, and the Philippines; then to defend Japan, Okinawa, Formosa, and the Philippines we needed the islands immediately off the mainland, plus Korea and South Vietnam. It seems likely that in Asia, there is still not an end to what more we must contest in order to keep what we have.

Mr. Morse went on to say that

> unless the killing of American troops in Southeast Asia is stopped quickly, domestic disunity is certain to increase because a foreign policy that conscripts our youth into military fodder to be consumed in an immoral and unjustifiable war will be repudiated by our people. It is being repudiated by increasing tens of thousands of our citizens, as it should be.

This was a reaffirmation of Mr. Morse's eloquent calls over the years for an enlightened foreign policy which would put a stop to our maintenance of a "military posture of dominance" in Asia and other parts of the world.

This is not a new theme. But the ideas that truly matter in society are often tattered with age. War and peace is a notable instance. Fearless, uninterrupted talk about it may yet be the only agency capable of bringing about man's release from his own follies, if not his doom.

Among the men in public life who are superbly knowledgeable in Far Eastern affairs is Senator Mike Mansfield of Montana. Ma-

[5] Alfred M. Landon Lecture, Kansas State University, Manhattan, March 10, 1969. Text furnished by Senator Mike Mansfield (Democrat, Montana), with permission for this reprint.

[6] For biographical note, see Appendix.

jority leader of the Senate, member of the Foreign Relations Committee, former professor of history and political science at Montana State University, and member of various commissions and delegations to European and Asian meetings, he combines a steely solicitude for facts and logic with a warm humanitarian concern for the deepening agonies of man. In his speechmaking he eschews flamboyance, theatrics, posturing. He is a matter-of-fact orator: serious, forthright, articulate, civil.

This characterization is exemplified in his lecture in the Alfred M. Landon series at Kansas State University in Manhattan. On March 10, 1969, he presented a detailed development showing that America, both by choice and error, has cast itself "in the role of Asian power." Originally we were, as he remarked, "an Atlantic-minded nation"; but through extensions of outposts and commitments in the Far East we now face in both directions. Accordingly, Mr. Mansfield called for a new "Pacific perspective" based upon a "spirit of cooperation and collaboration, free of attributes of dominance or condescension." The keynote, he said, must be mutuality. We have no other choice:

> We must make the effort to put our policies into that perspective. We will not only continue to live in the Pacific, we will also have to learn to live with the Pacific and the nations of its western reaches, basing our relations with its peoples—with the Chinese, Japanese, Filipinos, Koreans, Indonesians, and others—henceforth, on a profound respect for the equal dignity and worth of all.

We have been an Atlantic-minded nation and understandably so. Fourteen of the states border the Atlantic. The majority of our ancestors reached America via the Atlantic. Most of us follow religions of transatlantic origin. The languages that are learned in our schools are primarily those of the nations across the Atlantic. Americans who travel abroad usually begin their journeys by crossing the Atlantic. Fashions, architecture, routines of living in this nation all show strong influences from the opposite side of the ocean. We are, in short, preponderantly Atlantic by heredity, tradition, and proclivity.

However, the authority as well as the territory of the United States stops at the western edges of the ocean. The Atlantic has been a kind of sea barrier for us in the sense that the Pacific has not been. In the Pacific, not only do five states reach the ocean, but one of them—Hawaii—literally emerges from it. In addition, we have territories of various sizes, shapes, and legal relationships spread through its distant reaches. The Aleutian Islands which project towards the Soviet Union and Japan are part of the State of Alaska. American Samoa, Guam, Wake, Johnston, Midway and the Howland, Baker and Jarvis Islands are far-flung dependencies. The Canton and Enderbury Islands are an American-British condominium. The Trust Territory of the Pacific Islands has been administered by the United States since the end of the Second World War; it comprises over 2,000 islands and atolls which together total only 678 square miles of land but which are dispersed over 3 million square miles of ocean. World War II left a provisional American administration in Okinawa and the other Ryukyu Islands; there it has remained for a quarter of a century, almost within sight of the Asian mainland. More than a frontier, more than an avenue of communication and trade, the Pacific is a vast marine-arena within which lie states, territories, and dependencies appertaining in large part to the United States.

I would like to make clear that in referring to the Pacific, I do not include the Asian mainland or the waters immediately adjacent. On that mainland, there are no American possessions but there are more American forces than anywhere else in the world outside the United States. Not only is there the immense consignment in Vietnam but large American military contingents are also stationed in Thailand and South Korea. For the first time in history, we have deployed military power in mass along the whole arc of the Asian mainland.

In this manner, almost without realizing it, we have cast ourselves in the role of Asian power. We have extended the outposts of our Pacific power to China's borders. We have done so on the assumption that China is bent on military expansion and that it is essential for the United States to contain that expansion. That we have erred in the form of our response, even if the assumptions are accurate, is illustrated, in my judgment, by the war in Vietnam. The war has not contained China in any sense. Nor has it even decreased Chinese influence in Vietnam. If anything, it may be having the opposite effect.

What needs most to be learned from the tragic experience in Vietnam is that there is no national interest of the United States which requires us to perform the functions of an Asian power. On the contrary, it is as self-damaging as it is futile to presume that that role can be exercised by an outside power anywhere on the Asian landmass. The fact is that the nations of Asia are going to develop along economic and political lines which are determined by themselves. The development will spring from their history, philosophy, and tradition. It will be based on their human and material resources. It will reflect the political realities of their surroundings.

Nations outside the region, perhaps, can participate economically in limited ways in this process, but they cannot control the social evolution of Asia. What applies to other outside nations applies to us. We have never been a part of the Asian continent. We are not now. We will not be in the future.

However, we are a part of the Pacific, as I have already observed, and we will continue to be. Whether we will remain a Pacific power is not in question; we have no choice. What is at issue is our future role with respect to Asia. On that score, it seems to me, the character of our commitment is largely a matter of our choice. We were not forced, for example, into the present involvement in Vietnam. Largely by a pyramiding of successive unilateral declarations and acts, the commitment was built to its great dimensions. The choice was ours. By the same token, this nation, through the President, still retains, in my judgment, the capacity to increase, reduce, or even to dismantle that commitment by its own calculated decisions.

Whatever else may prove true of our future role in Asian affairs, I am persuaded that it will differ from the role we have played in the past. The postwar World War II era has ended, whether or not we recognize it. Whether or not we realize it, we are in a period of transition in our relations with the nations of the Western Pacific.

That such is the case is best illustrated by reference to Japan. Our relations with that nation have been relatively quiescent for many years. Time has brought changes in Japan which have now reached a point just short of crisis.

The cloud on the horizon is the U.S.-Japan security treaty. Under the terms of the treaty, beginning in 1970 either party may announce an intent to amend or terminate the agreement. As this date has drawn closer, the political debate in Japan over the treaty has grown in intensity. It has centered on two specific points.

The first is the question of the American bases in Japan —number, location and use. Among the Japanese, there has been a growing resentment of these bases. They are not uniformly regarded as sources of a benevolent American protection. Often, they are seen as symbols of excessive foreign influence as well as hazardous nuisances. Furthermore, U.S. military airfields, on occasion, act to disturb the populace, not only because they occupy scarce land, but also because they pose dangers of accidental explosions and crashes. In the case of naval bases there is, in Hiroshima-conscious Japan, the additional concern with the assumed danger of radiation whenever nuclear-powered U.S. vessels call at these facilities.

The second specific issue around which the debate has centered in Japan is the question of the Ryukyu Islands (notably Okinawa), which were an integral part of Japan before World War II. At the end of that conflict, the United States occupied these islands and has since administered them through the Defense Department. The Japanese peace treaty of 1951, however, left dangling, so to speak, certain matters pertaining to their final disposition. While the United States retained administrative control, Japan was not required to relinquish sovereignty. Moreover, this nation has since stated on more than one occasion that there is no question that Japan possesses "residual" sovereignty over the Ryukyus.

Nevertheless, the United States has converted Okinawa into a great military depot. Bases on the island are specifically exempted from certain restrictions which are in effect on similar U.S. installations in Japan proper. In 1960 the United States agreed that bases on the Japanese main islands cannot be used for "military combat operations" without the agreement of the Japanese government but by contrast the same inhibition is not in effect in Okinawa which has served as a staging area for the war in Vietnam and for B-52 bomber operations. Finally, there is a most fundamental difference: we have agreed not to store nuclear weapons in Japan proper; there is no such agreement respecting Okinawa.

The military bases relate to the larger issue of Japan's future military role in the Pacific. What is involved in this question is the continuance of a situation in which the primary responsibility for defending Japan, and indeed the entire Western Pacific, falls to the United States. Over the years, this state of affairs has cost us untold billions of dollars. Its persistence is now beginning to appear somewhat anachronistic a quarter of a century after World War II and with a Japan that is the third greatest industrial power in the world.

Many Japanese are restless under U.S. military surveillance of their homeland and adjacent waters. On the other hand, there is also a conflicting factor of Japanese anxiety that American military protection may be withdrawn. Out of the dichotomy has come a view that Japan should rearm beyond the modest "self-defense" forces which it possesses and assume a part of the defense functions which are now being discharged by this nation. The view has adherents not only in Japan but in certain quarters in the United States.

All of the issues which I have discussed so far have a significant characteristic in common: they are military matters. There are, of course, also nonmilitary matters in dispute between Japan and the United States as, for example, certain

barriers to trade and investment. The fact remains, nevertheless, that the main source of friction in U.S.-Japanese
relations, today, is to be found in disagreement over military
questions. I emphasize this point because there has been
some tendency to avoid public consideration of these matters in connection with foreign policy. Yet the questions are
fundamental. The future of the U.S.-Japanese relationship
will be very shaky, indeed, if we proceed to try to base it preponderantly on our military convenience in the Pacific, not-
withstanding the irritation and hostility which may be
caused thereby in Japan.

It seems to me there is a need for great alertness to changing Japanese attitudes respecting our military activities.
While some sentiment already exists in Japan for the re-
moval of all U.S. military bases, I do not think that that is
the dominant view. There is, rather, a general desire to see
a reduction in the number of U.S. bases in Japan. A prompt
response to this desire, I believe, not only would meet Japanese wishes but would also correspond to the interests of this
nation. Certainly, it would dovetail with our present effort
to reduce Federal expenditures and, in particular, expenditures abroad. In my judgment, it would also act, in timely
fashion, to preserve an accommodating tone in U.S.-Japanese
relations.

Indeed, I am persuaded that much of the growing controversy with Japan could be dispelled if it were simply stated
that we are prepared to abide by Japanese desires respecting
the bases. The installations are maintained at great cost to
this nation on the grounds of the contribution which they
make to Japanese security and, hence, indirectly to the security of the United States. If the bases have now ceased to
have that function in Japanese calculations, how can they
possibly serve a useful purpose in ours? They become, in fact,
a growing liability if they cause mounting friction between
this nation and the Japanese populace.

Whatever the sentiments on the question of American
bases in Japan, Okinawa is the looming issue in Japanese-

American relations. It is the lightning rod, so to speak, which has attracted most of the arguments, most of the protests, and most of the attention.

There is strong and growing pressure within Japan and Okinawa for the immediate repossession of full control over the Ryukyus. It seems to me that we have delayed a long time—perhaps too long—on this sensitive issue. Okinawa is Japanese; we have never claimed otherwise. I see no just or rational alternative other than to try to arrive at a fixed time-schedule for the progressive and prompt return of administrative control over the Ryukyu Islands to Japan. In restoring Japanese administrative control over Okinawa, moreover, it seems to me that there are also strong arguments against insisting on a "deal" which will permit the use of the military bases in ways which are not acceptable to the Japanese people.

There will be, I am sure, cries of anguish in some quarters at any significant modification of our right to unrestricted use of Okinawa. Nevertheless, entrenched parochial interests cannot be permitted to prevail in this critical matter. Okinawa is undoubtedly a great military convenience but it is by no means indispensable. The fact is that there have been enormous technological developments in the military field since World War II. We now have missiles which can carry nuclear weapons into space. We have planes which can carry them in the atmosphere over the ocean. We have ships which can carry them on the ocean, and submarines which can carry them under the ocean. We also have other bases in the Pacific—bases which are under unchallenged American sovereignty—where nuclear weapons can be stored and where Strategic Air Command planes with nuclear weapons may be based without question or complaint.

As I have already noted, the issues of the bases and Okinawa relate to the larger question of Japan's future military role. Here, too, it seems to me, that a greater sensitivity to Japanese popular sentiment is essential. It would appear particularly ill-advised for the United States to try to push the Japanese towards a new and expanded military role in the Western Pacific. To be sure, the Japanese may one day raise the present level of their self-defense forces. They may even, one day, amend their constitution in order to possess other than self-defense forces. Any such decisions, however, should result from Japanese political processes which reflect Japanese judgments of Japanese needs—judgments for which the Japanese accept full responsibility. They should not result from American pressures reflecting American judgments of American needs and, for which, this nation in the end will have to bear responsibility.

If the Japanese do not assume the military burdens which the U.S. would relinquish when the bases in Japan are reduced in number and those on Okinawa are restricted in use, some will ask: who will defend the Pacific? Presumably, it is fear of China which gives rise to this question. It does not follow, however, if the Chinese are bound on expansion, that they are capable of transpacific aggression. Indeed, President Nixon has made it clear that he does not buy the contention of some defense advisers that a "thin" antiballistic missile system is needed because of the Chinese threat.

A thrust of military power across the Pacific is quite a different matter from expansion on the Asian continent. Even in the latter case there is a difference of view as to the nature of Chinese continental pressure and what constitutes the principal danger to orderly progress in Asia. Among the nations of Southeast Asia, for example, it is commonplace to find that the threat of Chinese military aggression is rated a more remote menace than the immediate problems of economic underdevelopment and political instability which, in some cases, stem from internal economic disparities and in others from conflicts between two or more countries within the region.

These latter problems can hardly be met by U.S. defense outposts in the Western Pacific. Rather, their solution requires cooperation for constructive purposes among the Southeast Asian nations and with other nations outside the region. In fact, such cooperation has begun and it is taking two forms. First, there are groups of states within the region, such as the newly formed Association of Southeast Asian Nations. Second, there are regional organizations with outside members, such as the Asian Development Bank. The Bank includes European and North American subscribers whose modern resources can play an important, if peripheral, part in the progress of the Asian nations.

In this connection, there seems to me to be considerable merit in Japanese suggestions that the United States, Canada, Australia, New Zealand, and Japan should form a Pacific community to help developing countries. I should add, that in a grouping of this kind, Japan can play a most significant part. Indeed, in my judgment, it is in the sphere of economic development wherein lies Japan's principal potential for a contribution to the peace and progress of the Western Pacific.

I have talked of several facets of the situation in an effort to place the needs of our Asian policies in clearer perspective; of the distinction between a Pacific power which we have no choice but to be and an Asian power which we can and should choose not to be; of our military relations with Japan and the heat which is rising from the issues of the bases, Okinawa, and the overall Japanese role in the security of the Western Pacific; and, finally, of economic development in the Asian countries and the possibilities of cooperative aid. There are several other related questions which need to be touched on to complete this discussion. One concerns our relations with mainland China.

Strictly speaking, China is not of the Pacific but of Asia. Yet, the very vastness of China projects its relevance not only over the Asian mainland and the Pacific but, in fact, throughout the entire world. It is not possible to talk about the future of international peace, let alone about our future in the Pacific, without reference to the great nation which lies on its farther shore.

China will not remain forever, as is now the case, in substantial isolation. Its proper role is as a leading nation in the councils of the world. Sooner or later China will assume that place. It seems to me the Japanese have long since come to recognize that prospect. And there are indications that they are seeking to bridge the gap with China. Even if we could, there is no cause for this nation to impose obstacles of any kind—either spoken or unspoken—to increasing Japanese contacts with China. On the contrary, such efforts—whether in the economic, cultural, or political fields—might well be encouraged. They can serve not only Japan's needs for trade, they can contribute to clearing up a whole range of enigmas involving China and the security of the Western Pacific. In that fashion, they can be helpful in bringing about an enlightened approach to the building of a stable peace in that region.

For our part, and for much the same reasons, I see no purpose in imposing any special restrictions on the travel of Americans to China. Nor do I see any reason not to place trade with China in nonstrategic goods on the same basis as trade with the Soviet Union, Poland, and other Communist countries. For a decade and a half we have sought to maintain a rigid primary and secondary boycott of Chinese goods. The effort is unique in our history and it finds no parallel among the present practices of other nations with respect to China. In my view, we would be well advised to abandon this antiquated pursuit of China's downfall by economic warfare and treat with the Chinese in matters of trade as we treat with European Communist countries—no better and no worse.

It seems to me, the Nixon Administration's announced intention to reopen previous offers to exchange journalists, scientists, and scholars with China is well founded. The cancellation of the meeting in Warsaw on February 20, at which these offers were to be reiterated, is regrettable. One can only hope that another opportunity will soon present itself and, hopefully, that the official offers will be made and accepted.

Trade, travel, and cultural and scientific exchanges are relatively tangible issues in our relationship with China.

Hence, they seem to be more readily amenable to solution; perhaps, that is why current discussion of the relationship with China tends to concentrate on them. Similarly, the present debate is intensive on the questions of Chinese admission to the United Nations and U.S. diplomatic recognition of Peking. These issues, too, seem susceptible to clear solution. They are not, however, at the root of the difficulties. To try to resolve them at this point may be a useful intellectual exercise but it also tends to put the cart of the difficulty before the horse.

The fundamental problem of U.S.-Chinese relations is the status of Taiwan. It is a problem which is as complex as it is crucial. It is not an either-or issue. It is not really soluble, in an enduring sense, in terms of two Chinas as has been suggested in recent years because there are not two Chinas and the attempt to delineate them is synthetic. The fact is that China is a part of Taiwan and Taiwan is a part of China. Both Chinese governments which are agreed on little else are agreed on that score. The question is not whether the twain shall meet but when and in what circumstances. While we are not aloof from this question, the decisions which appertain thereto involve primarily the Chinese themselves—the Chinese of the mainland and the Chinese of Taiwan. Sooner or later the decisions will have to begin to be made. Only then will the other part of the Chinese puzzle—such questions as U.S. recognition and UN admission—fall into a rational place in our policies.

While I have spoken today principally about the United States, Japan, and China, two other major nations are of immediate concern. I refer to the Republic of the Philippines and to Indonesia.

There are signs of difficulties in our relations with the Philippines, principally in the field of trade and investment and with respect to U.S. military bases. In my judgment, however, none of the problems which confront us is of a nature as to be beyond reasonable solution in the light of the general cooperation which we have long enjoyed with the

Philippines. Yet it is precisely this basic cooperation which seems to me now to be in jeopardy. It is adversely affected by a vestigial tendency—a hangover from preindependence days—to continue to think almost automatically in terms of special economic privileges and concessions. Similarly in the field of foreign relations there is an inclination to expect that the policy of the Philippines government, inevitably, will mirror our own attitudes. Therefore, such departures as the recent Philippine initiation of contact with Communist countries seems somehow inimical to continued warm U.S.-Philippines relations. That is ironic inasmuch as we have long since had contact with most of these countries.

It is not a law of nature—it is an Aesopian fable—that familiarity must always breed contempt. A half century of familiarity which was crowned with the common sacrifices of World War II laid the basis not for a mutual contempt but for an enduring friendship between the Filipino and American people. It seems to me that we need to bestir ourselves now if this mutually valuable tie is not to be lost. Indeed, it would be my hope that the new Administration would give prompt attention to this matter.

To allow barriers of estrangement to be raised, by negligence or nonsense, is to admit a serious disability in our capacity to order our relations with other countries, notably those which have gained independence since World War II. After all, if we cannot hold the confidence, the friendship, and the respect of a people with whom we have been intimately associated for half a century, what can be expected with regard to other nations in Asia with which we have had little or no historic connection?

Indonesia is one such nation. Formerly the Dutch East Indies, this immense island chain was largely unknown to Americans during the colonial era. In the postindependence period, there has been a considerable contact but it has been uneven and unpredictable. In recent years, there has been a deterioration which, at times, has reached almost the point of outright mutual hostility. The pendulum apparently is now swinging and hope exists once again for a more agreeable situation.

It will take time, however, for us to form a balanced view of this enormous island-nation which in terms of population is the sixth largest in the world. It will take time, too, for Indonesia to emerge from its accumulated political and economic ills. The burden of the past is heavy and pervasive.

The United States can do little to speed up the development of a better association with Indonesia. Indeed in present circumstances the best policy is to accept our own limitations in this regard. To be sure, there are the gestures of goodwill which can be made in the form of technical, scientific, and educational cooperation. Moreover, through regional aid channels, such as I have already discussed, some assistance can be provided to Indonesia for economic development. That is a far cry, however, from self-delusive assumptions that by sending Americans to fight in Vietnam we have somehow saved Indonesia from communism or that the astute efforts of U.S. agencies and enough money in some miraculous fashion can act to delineate the emerging structure of the Indonesian nation.

Having described the problems which confront the United States in the Pacific, I feel that I have an obligation to close with a few general words of prescription. Almost fifty years of association with the Pacific—as a student, marine, teacher, and frequent visitor—prompt me to do so. A quarter of a century of political experience, on the other hand, impel me in the other direction. In these years of specializing in foreign relations both in the House of Representatives and in the Senate I have come to recognize the general absence of finality in the disposition of major international problems.

Nevertheless, I did remark at the outset that whatever our future in the Pacific, that future will be unlike the past. I am now under some compulsion to fill in details which sustain the general observation. The most fundamental new factor in the situation, as I see it, is the appearance of at least one new generation since my generation began to grapple with the post-World War II Asian situation and, in particular and with a singular lack of effectiveness, with the monumental upheaval of the Chinese revolution. This new generation is a source of hope for the future. It is a hope which derives largely from the interest young people now take in the affairs of the other side of the Pacific. That interest is more profound and far better informed than was the case two decades or more ago.

It used to be that in an Atlantic-minded nation the consideration of Asian questions was left largely to a relative handful of Americans, to "old Asian" or "old China hands," whose attitudes were churned out of a mixture of nineteenth century religious altruism, political idealism, cold-cash imperialism, and unscrupulous adventurism. World War II altered this mixture; the Korean War modified it further; and now Vietnam has changed it greatly. The attitudes which once held sway in this nation with respect to our relations with Asia and the Pacific have lost most of their relevance and much of their potency.

If there is to be a worthwhile future in the Pacific, it seems to me that U.S. policies for the problems of the Asian littoral will not be left in "old Asian hands." Rather they will take on the sense and sensitivity of "young American hands." The problems will be dealt with in a new spirit of cooperation and collaboration, free of attitudes of dominance or condescension. The keynote of a new policy for contemporary Asia, as I see it, is mutuality. Its characteristics will be mutual respect, mutual appreciation, and mutual forbearance.

For us there is no choice. We must make the effort to put our policies into that perspective. We will not only continue to live in the Pacific, we will also have to learn to live with the Pacific and the nations of its western reaches, basing our relations with its peoples—with the Chinese, Japanese, Filipinos, Koreans, Indonesians, and others—henceforth, on a profound respect for the equal dignity and worth of all.

POSTSCRIPTS TO ELECTORAL CHOICE

INAUGURAL ADDRESS [1]

RICHARD M. NIXON [2]

A pastime in which many students of oratory engage at four-year intervals is the selection of the best inaugural addresses delivered by American Presidents. While the choices are wide, a few favorites claim more than ordinary popularity. Among them are Thomas Jefferson's first address on March 4, 1801; Abraham Lincoln's first on March 4, 1861, and even more universally, the second on March 4, 1865; Woodrow Wilson's second on March 5, 1917; Franklin D. Roosevelt's first and third addresses on March 4, 1931, and January 20, 1941, respectively; and John F. Kennedy's widely heralded speech on January 20, 1961. During the preparation of his own address, President Richard M. Nixon surprised his assistants by naming James K. Polk's statement of March 4, 1845, as one of his favorites.

While it is doubtless true that inaugural speeches follow a built-in formula, they offer wide latitude for the exercise of rhetorical ingenuity. The diffuse outpouring of a Warren G. Harding is a sharply different note from the tight, succinct expression of an Abraham Lincoln. The rememberable phrases of a Franklin D. Roosevelt find no comparable parallels in the address of William Henry Harrison.

The primary function of the inaugural speech is to set the tone or temper of the incoming administration. Moreover, it announces the gauge of presidential hope and intention of accommodation to the urgencies of the time. It must assert the Executive's claim to leadership without extravagance of statement, without verbal professions of promise which may run counter to bruising realities.

Unlike Lyndon B. Johnson, President Nixon approached his oath with a narrow mandate from the people. He had received only slightly more than 40 per cent of the vote; and he had not fared well in gaining support from minority groups. Mindful of these conditions, and of the gnawing maladies in the nation, he

[1] The White House, Washington, D.C., January 20, 1969. Text furnished by the Office of the White House Press Secretary.

[2] For biographical note, see Appendix.

delivered a low-key address on January 20, 1969. His appeal was largely for peace and unity; his message, mildly sermonic, contained few programmatic notes. Instead of a summons to specific actions, his was a call for national dedication to broad principles and policies. It was a statement of personal commitment to the awesome task ahead. Perhaps that is precisely what the moment called for. If so, it made the simple response of a fourth-grade pupil in a Williamson, New York, school an adequate measure of the event: "[Mr. Nixon] made a very good speech. He has a big job."

Like many of his predecessors, Mr. Nixon drew quotation and paraphrase from the poets and statesmen: biblical patriarchs, Abraham Lincoln, Franklin D. Roosevelt, Woodrow Wilson, Archibald MacLeish. Admittedly, as *The Christian Science Monitor* observed editorially, "an Inaugural Address is words." But in this case, "the words were strong, calming, reassuring, as though [Mr. Nixon] knew, with Isaiah, that 'in quietness and in confidence shall be your strength.'"

Senator Dirksen, Mr. Chief Justice, Mr. Vice President, President Johnson, Vice President Humphrey, My Fellow Americans—and my fellow citizens of the world community:

I ask you to share with me today the majesty of this moment. In the orderly transfer of power, we celebrate the unity that keeps us free.

Each moment in history is a fleeting time, precious and unique. But some stand out as moments of beginning, in which courses are set that shape decades or centuries.

This can be such a moment.

Forces now are converging that make possible, for the first time, the hope that many of man's deepest aspirations can at last be realized. The spiraling pace of change allows us to contemplate, within our own lifetime, advances that once would have taken centuries.

In throwing wide the horizons of space, we have discovered new horizons on earth.

For the first time, because the people of the world want peace, and the leaders of the world are afraid of war, the times are on the side of peace.

Eight years from now America will celebrate its two hundredth anniversary as a nation. Within the lifetime of most people now living, mankind will celebrate that great new year which comes only once in a thousand years—the beginning of the Third Millennium.

What kind of a nation we will be, what kind of a world we will live in, whether we shape the future in the image of our hopes, is ours to determine by our actions and our choices.

The greatest honor history can bestow is the title of peacemaker. This honor now beckons America—the chance to help lead the world at last out of the valley of turmoil and onto that high ground of peace that man has dreamed of since the dawn of civilization.

If we succeed, generations to come will say of us now living that we mastered our moment, that we helped make the world safe for mankind.

This is our summons to greatness.

I believe the American people are ready to answer this call.

The second third of this century has been a time of proud achievement. We have made enormous strides in science and industry and agriculture. We have shared our wealth more broadly than ever. We have learned at last to manage a modern economy to assure its continued growth.

We have given freedom new reach. We have begun to make its promise real for black as well as for white.

We see the hope of tomorrow in the youth of today. I know America's youth. I believe in them. We can be proud that they are better educated, more committed, more passionately driven by conscience than any generation in our history.

No people has ever been so close to the achievement of a just and abundant society, or so possessed of the will to achieve it. And because our strengths are so great, we can afford to appraise our weaknesses with candor and to approach them with hope.

Standing in this same place a third of a century ago, Franklin Delano Roosevelt addressed a nation ravaged by depression and gripped in fear. He could say in surveying the nation's troubles: "They concern, thank God, only material things."

Our crisis today is in reverse.

We have found ourselves rich in goods, but ragged in spirit; reaching with magnificent precision for the moon, but falling into raucous discord on earth.

We are caught in war, wanting peace. We are torn by division, wanting unity. We see around us empty lives, wanting fulfillment. We see tasks that need doing, waiting for hands to do them.

To a crisis of the spirit, we need an answer of the spirit.

And to find that answer, we need only look within ourselves.

When we listen to "the better angels of our nature," we find that they celebrate the simple things, the basic things—such as goodness, decency, love, kindness.

Greatness comes in simple trappings.

The simple things are the ones most needed today if we are to surmount what divides us, and cement what unites us.

To lower our voices would be a simple thing.

In these difficult years, America has suffered from a fever of words; from inflated rhetoric that promises more than it can deliver; from angry rhetoric that fans discontents into hatreds; from bombastic rhetoric that postures instead of persuading.

We cannot learn from one another until we stop shouting at one another—until we speak quietly enough so that our words can be heard as well as our voices.

For its part, government will listen. We will strive to listen in new ways—to the voices of quiet anguish, the voices that speak without words, the voices of the heart—to the injured voices, the anxious voices, the voices that have despaired of being heard.

Those who have been left out, we will try to bring in.

Those left behind, we will help to catch up.

For all of our people, we will set as our goal the decent order that makes progress possible and our lives secure.

As we reach toward our hopes, our task is to build on what has gone before—not turning away from the old, but turning toward the new.

In this past third of a century, government has passed more laws, spent more money, initiated more programs, than in all our previous history.

In pursuing our goals of full employment, better housing, excellence in education; in rebuilding our cities and improving our rural areas; in protecting our environment and enhancing the quality of life; in all these and more, we will and must press urgently forward.

We shall plan now for the day when our wealth can be transferred from the destruction of war abroad to the urgent needs of our people at home.

The American dream does not come to those who fall asleep.

But we are approaching the limits of what government alone can do.

Our greatest need now is to reach beyond government, to enlist the legions of the concerned and the committed.

What has to be done, has to be done by government and people together or it will not be done at all. The lesson of past agony is that without the people we can do nothing; with the people we can do everything.

To match the magnitude of our tasks, we need the energies of our people—enlisted not only in grand enterprises, but more importantly in those small, splendid efforts that make headlines in the neighborhood newspaper instead of the national journal.

With these, we can build a great cathedral of the spirit— each of us raising it one stone at a time, as he reaches out to his neighbor, helping, caring, doing.

I do not offer a life of uninspiring ease. I do not call for a life of grim sacrifice. I ask you to join in a high adventure

—one as rich as humanity itself, and exciting as the times we live in.

The essence of freedom is that each of us shares in the shaping of his own destiny.

Until he has been part of a cause larger than himself, no man is truly whole.

The way to fulfillment is in the use of our talents. We achieve nobility in the spirit that inspires that use.

As we measure what can be done, we shall promise only what we know we can produce, but as we chart our goals, we shall be lifted by our dreams.

No man can be fully free while his neighbor is not. To go forward at all is to go forward together.

This means black and white together, as one nation, not two. The laws have caught up with our conscience. What remains is to give life to what is in the law: to insure at last that as all are born equal in dignity before God, all are born equal in dignity before man.

As we learn to go forward together at home, let us also seek to go forward together with all mankind.

Let us take as our goal: where peace is unknown, make it welcome; where peace is fragile, make it strong; where peace is temporary, make it permanent.

After a period of confrontation, we are entering an era of negotiation.

Let all nations know that during this Administration our lines of communication will be open.

We seek an open world—open to ideas, open to the exchange of goods and people, a world in which no people, great or small, will live in angry isolation.

We cannot expect to make everyone our friend, but we can try to make no one our enemy.

Those who would be our adversaries, we invite to a peaceful competition—not in conquering territory or extending dominion, but in enriching the life of man.

As we explore the reaches of space, let us go to the new worlds together—not as new worlds to be conquered, but as a new adventure to be shared.

With those who are willing to join, let us cooperate to reduce the burden of arms, to strengthen the structure of peace, to lift up the poor and the hungry.

But to all those who would be tempted by weakness, let us leave no doubt that we will be as strong as we need to be for as long as we need to be.

Over the past twenty years, since I first came to this capital as a freshman congressman, I have visited most of the nations of the world. I have come to know the leaders of the world, and the great forces, the hatreds, the fears that divide the world.

I know that peace does not come through wishing for it— that there is no substitute for days and even years of patient and prolonged diplomacy.

I also know the people of the world.

I have seen the hunger of a homeless child, the pain of a man wounded in battle, the grief of a mother who has lost her son. I know these have no ideology, no race.

I know America. I know the heart of America is good.

I speak from my own heart, and the heart of my country, the deep concern we have for those who suffer, and those who sorrow.

I have taken an oath today in the presence of God and my countrymen to uphold and defend the Constitution of the United States. To that oath I now add this sacred commitment: I shall consecrate my office, my energies, and all the wisdom I can summon to the cause of peace among nations.

Let this message be heard by strong and weak alike:

The peace we seek—the peace we seek to win—is not victory over any other people, but the peace that comes "with healing in its wings"; with compassion for those who have suffered; with understanding for those who have opposed us; with the opportunity for all the peoples of this earth to choose their own destiny.

Only a few short weeks ago we shared the glory of man's first sight of the world as God sees it, as a single sphere reflecting light in the darkness.

As the Apollo astronauts flew over the moon's gray surface on Christmas eve, they spoke to us of the beauty of earth —and in that voice so clear across the lunar distance, we heard them invoke God's blessing on its goodness.

In that moment, their view from the moon moved poet Archibald MacLeish to write: "To see the earth as it truly is, small and blue and beautiful in that eternal silence where it floats, is to see ourselves as riders on the Earth together, brothers in that bright loveliness in the eternal cold— brothers who know now they are truly brothers."

In that moment of surpassing technological triumph, men turned their thoughts toward home and humanity—seeing in that far perspective that man's destiny on earth is not divisible; telling us that however far we reach into the cosmos, our destiny lies not in the stars but on earth itself, in our own hands, in our own hearts.

We have endured a long night of the American spirit. But as our eyes catch the dimness of the first rays of dawn, let us not curse the remaining dark. Let us gather the light.

Our destiny offers not the cup of despair, but the chalice of opportunity. So let us seize it not in fear, but in gladness— and, "riders on the Earth together," let us go forward, firm in our faith, steadfast in our purpose, cautious of the dangers; but sustained by our confidence in the will of God and the promise of man.

A MATTER OF DOUBT AND GRAVE CONCERN [3]

HAROLD F. HARDING [4]

At four-year intervals since 1948, papers have appeared in the *Quarterly Journal of Speech* assessing the rhetorical skills and methods of the major candidates for the presidency. Initiated by Harold F. Harding when he was editor of the publication, this series has provided keen insights and discerning critiques of the men, the issues, and the campaigns in which the art of oratory has played a productive and, conceivably in some instances, a crucial role.

Observers of the political scene do not agree of course on how much influence, if any, campaign oratory exerts in shaping the decisions of the voters. A substantial part of the candidates' spoken appeal is by radio and television; and despite the refinements of those media, they are still great changes from personal engagements in open meetings. Some ten years ago, Paul H. Douglas, then senator (Democrat) from Illinois, defended campaign speaking against the charge that it was a waste of time. But he was thinking largely of personal appearances before small groups. "With all their imperfections," Senator Douglas wrote, "campaign speeches [delivered before small groups] contribute to the open dialogue on questions upon which wise public decisions depend."

In the talk reprinted below, Harold F. Harding, a veteran writer and speaker on presidential elections, shared with his listeners the results of a poll which he conducted during the 1968 campaign largely for his own satisfaction and according to his own ground rules. Near the end of his analysis he asked the critical question: Was the campaign worth the quarter of a billion dollars which it allegedly cost? His answer was unhesitating: "as an educational process to enable voters to make good choices—emphatically No."

Dr. Harding was for many years a professor of speech at Ohio State University. Currently he is Benedict Professor of Speech at the University of Texas, El Paso. He delivered this address at a sectional meeting on Contemporary Public Address of the Speech Association of America in Chicago on December 30, 1968.

[3] Address delivered at a sectional meeting of the Speech Association of America, Chicago, December 30, 1968. Text furnished by Professor Harding, with permission for this reprint.

[4] For biographical note, see Appendix.

I have earned my living for years by telling students that if they spoke well they could persuade juries, sell stocks and bonds, and even marry a beautiful girl or a handsome husband. Now in my after-coffee-liqueur years I find in politics, at least, it isn't so. I've come to the reluctant conclusion that campaign speeches have little to do with the way a voter mysteriously *decides* which candidate to vote for, or as may often be the case—to vote *against*.

I've learned this sad fact of life, late in life, from persons who ought to know—United States senators and professors of speech. I had assumed they were knowledgeable about the presidential candidates and their ability to explain the issues. So last September and October I ran my own private Gallup poll, asking three questions:

1. Which man will you vote for?

2. Does his ability to explain the issues influence your decision?

3. If not, what did make you decide?

I don't intend to give you precise data because the professional polltakers would probably find fault with my methods—which are nonscientific. You would naturally expect Republican senators to vote for Nixon and Democrats for Humphrey and you are right. You would naturally expect professors of speech to attach great importance to a candidate's ability to speak. But no, you are wrong, I've been told by enough senators and enough professors of speech to convince me that speaking may have little or nothing to do with the way you actually decide to vote. Or at least the way they decide.

Out of 45 senators from whom I had usable replies 30 said that they were voting on the basis of party loyalty, 15 said that they had known the candidate, been friends with him, or believed him best qualified, and 25 added or intimated that speaking had nothing to do with their decisions. In fact the answers to my third question, "On what basis did you decide," were vague and almost noncommittal. I am a little ashamed to tell my students what the senators said.

With professors of speech I found about half of 60 usable answers saying that the persons were having a hard time to make up their minds this year. Some were going to take a walk and not vote at all. Some admitted they were going to vote largely for the party. Some said Humphrey's earlier record was the basis, others said it was his lack of clear stands that made them dislike Humphrey during the campaign. Practically none said they were voting because of Humphrey's readiness or ability to explain the current issues. About the same proportion said the same about Nixon.

What can we conclude? The evasiveness of the discussion of campaign issues in 1968 irritated many voters. It alienated some to go over to Wallace. For others the failure to discuss issues made no difference.

Perhaps the dissatisfaction of voters in 1968 shows up best in the startling fact that only 60 per cent of those eligible this year actually cast their ballots. This was down from 62 per cent in 1964 and 63 per cent in 1960. Three per cent of the 120 million persons of voting age is 3.6 million, a very sizable number.

The paradox of the campaign stems from two or three words: *apathy* and *switching* or *splitting*. As many as 19 million voters, Dr. Gallup, reports "said that they had at some point during the campaign intended to vote for a candidate other than the one they supported on November 5, 54 per cent of all the voters said they had split their tickets this year. But most significantly one voter in four said that, even two weeks before the election, he had not definitely made up his mind how he would vote." Earlier reports at convention times had reduced the undecideds this year to about 5 per cent or 7 per cent. The interpretation we make is that the events of the last weeks of the campaign made two or three times as many voters *undecided*—in relation to, say, August 1968. It seems to run counter to what I argued earlier that speaking didn't matter. But I'm not sure that the speaking did the trick. It would appear that a great soul-searching took place in the last two weeks. Perhaps some of those enchanted with George Wallace became disenchanted. Some who were anti-Humphrey or only lukewarm came over to his side. Some who were solidly for Nixon may have switched when the prospect of Spiro Agnew as a President loomed up before them. Similarly, many who were anti-Humphrey were enthusiastic about Senator Muskie and voted for Humphrey because they knew Muskie would make a good President. In any event, the fact that Muskie had a full-fledged role in the final Democratic TV show the night before election and that Agnew was not even on stage seems to bear out that Nixon had doubts about the image Agnew had created. Even since the election Governor Agnew has had a bad press caused by some of his inept remarks.

You remember too how Mr. Nixon gave a hard-sell talk about Ted Agnew when he presented his cabinet over TV to the American people on December 11th. You got the impression that Ted Agnew was going to run National Security Council meetings and Cabinet sessions when Mr. Nixon was away or busy, that he was going to deal directly with the governors or this or that group, that his role would greatly expand from those of Messrs. Nixon and Johnson as Vice Presidents. In fact, there would be little time left for the usual vice presidential function of presiding at ceremonies. Or, to put the matter another way, wherever Mr. Agnew appears it will be a *ceremony*. One of the dictionary meanings of that word is "an action performed only formally with no deep significance."

Both Nixon and Humphrey are ex-college debaters. They have been debating before audiences most of their adult lives. But this year Mr. Nixon refused to debate on TV against Mr. Humphrey. Whereas, Humphrey had for years been appearing on "Meet the Press," "Face the Nation," and "Issues and Answers," Mr. Nixon carefully avoided these programs in 1967 and 1968 and even earlier. Why was he so chicken-hearted? On May 13, 1968, Mr. Raymond E. Price, special assistant/speech writer assured me by letter that Mr. Nixon "meant what he said in that March 28th address about wanting a higher level of debate and discussion" and that "he would be willing to debate his Democratic opponent, whoever that turns out to be."

On November 28, 1967, Mr. Nixon was quoted in a New York *Times* interview with Warren Weaver, Jr., as saying "I believe there should be debates" and that "my [Nixon's] strength lies in the grasp of the issues and not the grasp of the hand."

It is true that L.B.J. refused to debate Barry Goldwater in 1964 but neither he nor Goldwater worried much about TV before that election.

Whether Nixon lost votes because he refused TV debates with Humphrey in 1968 will be discussed for some time. The fact remains that Mr. Nixon won by a slim popular plurality and it can be argued that not many persons were influenced one way or another by Nixon's refusal to debate this year.

It can also be argued that since Nixon "lost" his TV debates with Kennedy in 1960 he was taking no chances this year.

The campaign speaking this year was not really on the issue/problem—solution-offered basis that thinking voters hoped for. There were few speeches of real substance. Two of Mr. Nixon's were above the ordinary. The one on the office of the presidency, on September 20th, written by Raymond K. Price was thought provoking. Patrick Buchanan wrote "Order and Justice under Law" which Mr. Nixon spoke on September 30th and it was better than anything Mr. Nixon wrote including his acceptance speech. Mostly, Americans heard the speech Nixon has been giving for years and years.

Mr. Humphrey was a critic's nightmare. He spoke too often, too long, too vaguely, and often without much seeming conviction. True, he got better toward the end of the campaign and, as some believe, may have won if the election was held on November 12th.

But all this is conjecture. What we know about the 1968 campaign may be summed up briefly:

1. Richard Nixon was really running against L.B.J. and his conduct of the Vietnam War. Millions were against war. They voted for Nixon thinking he would end the war.

2. The Democratic party's organization was weak, without adequate funds, started late, was always on the defensive, and simply could not match the smooth-performing Nixon machine.

3. George Wallace lost his steam in the last three weeks but gained five states and forty-five electoral votes. He has probably hurt the regular Democratic organization in all Southern states for some years to come.

4. The time-for-a-change argument was the clincher for those on the line trying to decide. It helped more than anything to make up minds. Any Republican nominee would have benefited by this argument. It put Nixon over.

5. L.B.J.'s support of Humphrey late in the campaign probably helped in Texas if nowhere else. If President Johnson had vigorously campaigned for Humphrey, Nixon's plurality may have been greater.

6. Whether the people who elected Nixon constitute the Responsible Electorate in V. O. Key's sense will be determined only after Mr. Nixon has been at his desk for some months—perhaps four full years. The fact that the final vote was so close and that there was so much last-minute deciding might argue that confusion, doubt, and half-satisfaction were the order of the day.

7. Certainly the fact that only 60 per cent of those eligible actually voted argues for much indecision. When we consider that Nixon's plurality is 43 per cent of 72 million voters it means that three out of four American citizens are unhappy with him, or don't really care, or had other reasons for staying away from the polls on Election Day. In any

business organization where only one quarter of the workers support the boss the morale is not very high.

Any scholar interested in the technical features of rhetoric will have a happy hunting ground in the 1968 campaign speeches. They are rich in figures of speech and figures of thought—most of which the writers and speakers are unaware of. They simply fell into the habit of doing what comes naturally in campaign oratory. Without attempting to document by speech and date, here are a few examples:

1. Both presidential nominees, and especially Mr. Wallace of the American Independent party: the use of *hyperbole,* both exaggerated and extravagant terms. Also by Mr. Wallace constant disparagement of his opponents' arguments—called *diasyrmus.*

2. All six main speakers and especially Governor Agnew: *metastasis,* a passing over an issue quickly and lightly.

3. Vice President Humphrey especially: *macrologia,* long-winded speaking.

4. Mr. Nixon especially: *heterogenium,* an irrelevant answer to distract attention.

5. Mr. Humphrey on rare occasions: *paramologia,* conceding a point usually to strengthen his own argument.

6. General LeMay on his first press conference: *parrhesia,* very frank and candid speaking.

7. Senator Muskie on most occasions: *digestion,* an orderly enumeration of the points he wishes to discuss.

8. Governor Wallace especially: *poicologia,* awkward and ungrammatical sentences.

9. Mr. Nixon especially: *occupatio,* an effort to emphasize a point by deliberately seeming to pass over it—usually confused by the expression "Let me make this point perfectly clear."

10. And again Mr. Nixon: *interpretatione,* the repetition of an idea in different words. Although this rhetorical device is classified as an ornament, in Mr. Nixon's case after

eight years of running for the presidency it became not
energia, clear and vivid description, but on occasion its opposite, and often boring. The President-elect as a campaign
speaker, will not be recalled for his memorable phrases and
terse sayings.

The 1968 campaign cost more than $250 million. The
presidential candidates spent $55 million. Was it worth it?
As entertainment, No; as pseudo event, Yes; as an educational process to enable voters to make good choices—emphatically No.

Pericles defined the statesman as the man who knows the
proper policy, has the ability to expound it, and "who moreover is not only a patriot but an honest one." Mr. Nixon and
Mr. Agnew amply proved themselves to be clever politicians
in the 1968 campaign. Whether they can by the use of their
rhetoric prove themselves worthy of the definition of Pericles
in the four years ahead remains a matter of doubt and of
grave concern. To each I say in the words of St. Matthew,
chapter 26, verse 73, "Thy speech bewrayeth thee."

VIEWS ON THE STRUGGLES FOR EQUALITY

THIS IS OUR QUEST: TO FIGHT FOR THE RIGHT [1]

ARMANDO M. RODRIGUEZ [2]

In the Godkin Lectures at Harvard University on March 25, 1969, John W. Gardner, head of the Urban Coalition, quoted a passage from Isaiah in which the angry Jehovah cried out: "Make the heart of the people fat." "He intended it," said Mr. Gardner, "as a prelude to desolation, and so it will always be." But perhaps, Gardner continued, we were in greater danger "when we were less worried." Now that vast numbers of citizens appreciate the dimension of our anguish, we might "even be on the mend." He insisted, however, that the safe and proper way out of our dilemmas could come only through our "courage to look honestly at evil where evil exists," "to forswear hypocrisy," and "to call injustice and dishonor by their right names."

Leaders of minority groups in America have been voicing the same themes. In general, they have expressed a deep faith in equal educational opportunities as at least partial correctives of their people's distress. Hence the rightfully insistent calls for new thrusts in education for the blacks, the Indians, and the Hispanos. An eloquent call for a reassessment of educational policy and practice, especially as it concerns Mexican-Americans, is sounded in the speech below by Armando M. Rodriguez, a former teacher and administrator in the San Diego public schools and currently the head of the Mexican-American Affairs Unit of the Department of Health, Education, and Welfare. Appearing as the keynote speaker at the first meeting of MAYA (Mexican-American Youth Adelante) at the University of Colorado, Boulder, on May 8, 1969, Mr. Rodriguez asserted that the "melting-pot ideology that we speak of so proudly has not produced a moral climate in which all citizens are accepted on the basis of individual worth."

The real problem in our society today, and therefore the real problem in education [he remarked], is not the Negro problem nor the Mexican-American problem nor the Puerto

[1] Speech delivered at the first annual meeting of Mexican-American Youth Adelante, University of Colorado, Boulder, May 8, 1969. Text furnished by Mr. Rodriguez, with permission for this reprint.

[2] For biographical note, see Appendix.

Rican problem—it is the Anglo point-of-view problem. This point of view determines what happens in the school—what emphasis will be given or denied racial, cultural and language values. It is this point of view that through educational activities, social relations in the school, through the subtle, but devastating actions of education personnel, tells youngsters that they are not beautiful because they are different. This is the process that systematically makes it clear that this different youngster is unworthy and unwanted—and so are his parents.

The schools, Mr. Rodriguez declared, fail to "reflect the needs of today's youth. And this failure can be traced directly to the prevailing point of view that to be American is to erase all cultural identity through an education 'brainwash.' "

It is a privilege for me to be the keynote speaker at the first annual Mexican-American Youth Adelante Conference. I would like to congratulate the United Mexican-American Students, the University of Colorado and the Great Western Sugar Foundation for their interest in promoting the education of the Spanish-speaking youth of Colorado. It is through education that we will find the knowledge, the strength, the inspiration to fully realize our goals, our dreams, in this land of opportunity. First, we have to recognize that we are full-fledged Americans with the same rights and privileges as any other American. We have to understand who we are, what our historical past is, our surroundings, our weaknesses, our assets. We are here to discuss the problems of Mexican-American youth of the Southwest and in particular Colorado. We are here to discuss what help can be given to assist you in your higher education. We are hopeful that this conference will benefit you in promoting your educational aspirations.

It would be well to clarify the hyphenated term *Mexican-American* as herein to include an ethnic as well as a national concept describing the Spanish-speaking group of Mexican ancestry. This obviates the problem as to when his parents arrived in this country or where he may live.

There are those who raise the academic question of denying belonging to this ethnic group. Fortunately, history

cannot be denied or changed by wishful thinking of wanting
to be different. What difference does it make if a group
migrated to this country some thirty years ago or [was] in-
cluded as an integral social unit in the territory ceded to the
United States by Mexico at the Treaty of Guadalupe in
1848? The people and culture found in what is now the
Southwest were but an extension at this particular period
of the Mexican nation. Therefore, for all practical educational purposes, and if we are to think in terms of this ethni-
cal and national concept, the Mexican-American is a well-
defined social group whose ethos and cultural pattern differ
very little from Texas to California.

We must recognize that the Mexican-American is a reality. Many of you represent families who have been in this
territory for more than four centuries. Unfortunately, in
many parts of the Southwest, the Mexican-American is still
not considered a full-fledged citizen. Foreign immigrants to
the United States, particularly immigrants from northern
European countries, came to be referred to as Americans
within one or two generations. In the American Southwest,
however, a different situation exists. When Texas became
part of the United States, for example, Texans became citizens of the United States and were thereafter, called Americans. Mexican-Texans remained, and still are, in the everyday language of Texans, Mexicans rather than Americans.
Mexican does not properly describe those whose residence
north of the Rio Grande predates the existence of both Mexico and the United States as nations.

But it is less the geographical inaccuracy of the term
Mexican that invites comment than the meaning with which
the term is invested. As used and understood in the Southwest, *Mexican* is a descriptive term and carries with it an
entire complex of moral and physical attributes. It excludes
such commonplace notions of Americanism as godliness,
cleanliness, a sense of justice and fair play, Yankee know-
how. This may be denied, but proof that *Mexican* is used as

a disparaging term lies in the fact of its careful avoidance on the part of those who do not at the moment wish to offend.

The term *Mexican-American* ostensibly bestows a measure of Americanism on the recipient, yet balks at acknowledging unqualified American citizenship. Another alternative, prompted sometimes by misled notions of tact or kindness, sometimes by irony, is *Spanish*. If *Mexican* is geographically inaccurate, *Spanish* is even more inaccurate: there are relatively few Spaniards in the United States, and those that are here, by virtue of education or by virtue of being Europeans, generally move in higher circles than so-called Mexicans. We do not call Canadians *English,* nor Brazilians *Portuguese.* Yet we use *Spanish* in spite of its obvious inaccuracy and in tribute to the *evocative* power of *Mexican.* The tragedy is that many *Mexicans* resort to the same hypocrisy: bona fide Americans in every sense other than name, they assent to the stigma of *Mexican* by their disavowal of it. Tacitly, they concur with their detractors—not of their own choice, of course, but generations of conditioning has convinced them that they are indeed as the dominant society has portrayed them: different and inferior, unworthy of sharing the name *American.*

Popular American usage does not expressly distinguish between the Mexican national and the American-born citizen of more or less remote Mexican ancestry. The popular imagination mixes them both into a stereotype that is at once quaint and threatening. Across the length of the United States, the symbol of the Mexican is the peon, asleep against the wall of his adobe hut or at the foot of the saguaro cactus. At best he wears only sandals. He is lazy and given to putting things off until *mañana.* This picturesque fellow and his inevitable burro adorn the menus and neon signs of restaurants and motels all across the United States. At some point in his life, the peon wakes up, takes a drink of tequila, puts on his wide-brimmed sombrero, and emigrates to the United States —by swimming across the Rio Grande, of course. Once here, he loses his picturesque and harmless ways and becomes sinister: he is now proud and hotblooded, easily offended, intensely jealous, a drinker, cruel.

The myth of the lazy, jealous, passive, fatalistic Mexican is perpetuated in literature in such books as *Tortilla Flat, Rio Grande, The Oregon Trail.* In a *Treasury of American Folklore,* edited by B. A. Botkin, there is the following celebrated peroration, attributed to Judge Roy Bean, "The Law West of the Pecos":

> Carlos Robles, you have been tried by twelve true and good men, not men of yore peers, but as high above you as heaven is of hell, and they've said you're guilty of rustlin' cattle. Time will pass and seasons will come and go; spring with its wavin' green grass and heaps of sweet-smelling flowers on every hill and in every dale. Then will come sultry summer, with her shimmerin' heatwaves on the baked horizon; and fall, with her yeller harvest-moon and the hills growing brown and golden under a sinking sun; and finally winter, with its bitin' whinin' wind, and the land will be mantled with snow. But you won't be here to see any of 'em, Carlos Robles; not by a dam' sight, because it's the order of this court that you be took to the nearest tree and hanged by the neck till you're dead, dead, dead, you olive-colored son-of-a-billy-goat!

The prisoner, it is said, did not know a word of English, and missed the flavor of Roy Bean's oratory.

Only rarely in American literature of the Southwest does one encounter a portrayal of Mexicans that is both sympathetic and unsentimental. One sympathizer was Bret Harte. In a short story entitled, "The Devotion of Enriquez," Harte's sympathetic treatment of Mexicans is probably due, at least in part, to the fact that he sets his story in California at a time when Mexicans still held large tracts of land and mixed socially with the newer Californians. Mark Twain, too, had a brief word to say about Mexicans and he shared with Bret Harte an open admiration for their horsemanship. Despite the fact that it is in this area of horsemanship and horseraising that the Mexican contributed so much to the American West, Mark Twain's admiration has few echoes in later literature. Nevertheless, the Mexican horseman left his mark on the everyday English of the West: *bronco, lariat, lasso, rodeo, mustang, buckaroo.*

Yet, in spite of broncos and buckaroos, in spite of place names, in spite of architectural and musical influences, in spite of the millions of people who are a living reminder of the part that Spain and Mexico played in forming the character of the Southwest—in spite of all this, the American Mexican is an alien, unknown in his own land. Our history and culture are either ignored or romanticized. The Mexican is pictured on the one hand as the peon, who, hat in hand, holds the reins for the rich rancher in the movies, or is the Frito Bandito on TV. On the other hand, he is the glamorous *hidalgo,* the ambassador of goodwill for the city of San Diego and a participant in the Rose Bowl Parade. Between the fanciful extremes of the peon and the hidalgo is the ordinary American Mexican. Probably the most telling observation ever to be printed about the Mexican came from the pages of *Newsweek* (May 23, 1966): "We're the best-kept secret in America."

The secret is kept against considerable odds. There is, for example, the visibility of the Mexican, which, paradoxically, works against him: he is easily identified and, once identified, easily categorized and ignored. It is a complaint of Mexicans that they are seen only when they do wrong; otherwise, they don't exist—they are secret. In the words of a recent television special report (April 20, 1969), they are the "Invisible Minority." It is this nonexistence within American society that gives the Mexican the "furtive and uneasy look" that Octavio Paz perceived in the *pachucos* of Los Angeles in his book *El Laberinto de la Soledad.* The Mexican-American is neither truly American nor truly Mexican; he is suspended between the two cultures, neither of which claims him. As a result, he withdraws into himself and away from the larger society. An observation similar to that of Octavio Paz is made by Jack London in a short story entitled, "The Mexican." The hero of the story is a young Mexican boy in the United States as an alien; the reactions that he provokes in those about him have a significance beyond the limits of the story itself; "And still they could not bring themselves to like him.

They did not know him. His ways were not theirs. He gave no confidence. He repelled all probing."

This furtive, secretive air is adopted early in life. Shortly after entering the primary grades, the Mexican child begins to realize that he is different and that this difference is taken by society at large as a sign of inferiority. And it is not only his schoolmates that teach him: frequently the teachers themselves betray an ill-disguised contempt for the schools and neighborhoods in which they work. The opinions of the teacher are seconded by history books, wherein the youngsters read of the cruelty of the Spaniard toward the Indians, of the Spaniard's greed for gold, of the Spanish Inquisition, of Mexican bandits, and of the massacre of the Alamo.

The result of this kind of teaching, or lack of teaching, by school and society is that Mexican youngsters are kept ignorant of the contribution that their forebears made to the so-called winning of the West. At a time when they should be learning pride in their history and in their own peculiar kind of Americanism, these children are made to feel that they do not rightly participate in the American enterprise, that they are intruders in their own land. Mexican-American children can do and do well scholastically, but only in schools that not only help them adjust to Anglo society but also foster pride in their origin, history, culture, and bilingual background. A high school girl from the barrio in East Los Angeles said:

We look for others like ourselves in these history books, for something to be proud of for being a Mexican, and all we see in books, magazines, films, and TV shows are stereotypes of a dark, dirty, smelly man with a tequila bottle in one hand, a dripping taco in the other, a sarape wrapped around him, and a big sombrero. An area for immediate and forceful action in our quest to fight for the right is in the use of the negative image of the *Chicano* in advertising. I need not identify the specific cases— there are too many to enumerate. Let's get rid of them, or organize a massive boycott of these products.

Mexican-Americans cannot be described according to a simplistic formula, despite the strident assertions made by social scientists, assertions that insist upon the antiquated idea of a bipolar process of change beginning at one point and leading all Mexican-Americans in the same direction, like sheep—from stagnant fatalism to assimilation and creativity. But actual history itself reveals this formulation to be a grand hoax, a blatant lie. Witness the seemingly endless decades of labor conflict initiated by Mexicans and Mexican-Americans—conflict which involved literally tens of thousands of people of Mexican descent and which at one time spread to eight different states in the nation—conflict which was met with massive military counteraction. Social scientists have never asked themselves just why such massive military action was necessary in order to deal with a resigned, passive, fatalistic, nongoal-oriented people with lax habits and no plans for the future. The concept of the traditional culture as presently used by social scientists must be totally dropped. Instead, the concept of the historical culture must be adopted. Unfortunately, many of these books have become the authoritative sources of information about Mexican-Americans for a wide variety of institutional agencies, from schools of medicine, departments of social welfare, to departments of employment and other governmental agencies. In this way, thousands upon thousands of people, many of them Mexican-Americans themselves, have been indoctrinated with the historically perverted notion that Mexican-Americans are a historical people who have had no history except that of a long and tedious siesta.

Despite the constant reinforcement of his native culture at every turn, and the powerful forces that pull him in two directions, the Mexican-American has his loyalty to this country. His loyalty is unquestionably to the Stars and Stripes, as an enviable military record demonstrates in Vietnam. Mexican-Americans have never had a turncoat—not even in the Korean War. We won more Medals of Honor during World War II than any other ethnic group. The late U.S. Senator Chavez from New Mexico once said:

At the time of war we are called "the great patriotic Americans," and during elections politicians call us "the great Spanish-speaking community of America." When we ask for jobs we are called "those damn Mexicans!"

If, then, Mexican-Americans are not Americans, what are they? What is an American? Regardless of what we call ourselves or are called: *coloniales, manitos, hispanos, mexicanos, espanoles,* Spanish-American, Mexican-American, Latin American, we are Americans. Who is more American? Carlos Garcia whose ancestors came aboard the Santa Maria or Paul Smith whose forebears arrived on the Mayflower? We should have pride of our Hispanic-Mexican background. History in this continent predated the arrival of Columbus and the Pilgrims. We still need to give full account of the contributions of the Mayan and Aztec civilizations. We should know that the first printing press was established in Mexico City and that the University of Mexico was founded one hundred years before Harvard University. We are proud of being Americans, we have roots in this continent. Who should be ashamed of this past? If you are ashamed of being what you are, then you are ashamed of being a man. The important thing is that you are accepted and respected. This is our fight, our quest. We must correct it.

Who am I? [asks a young Mexican-American high school student]. I am a product of myself. I am a product of you and my ancestors. We came to California long before the Pilgrims landed at Plymouth Rock. We settled California, the southwestern part of the United States including the states of Arizona, New Mexico, Colorado and Texas. We built the missions, we cultivated the ranches. We were at the Alamo, in Texas, both inside and outside. You know we owned California—that is, until gold was found here. Who am I? I'm a human being. I have the same hopes that you do, the same fears, the same drives, same desires, same concerns, same abilities; and I want the same chance that you have to be an individual. Who am I? In reality I am who you want me to be.

This inner struggle of the Mexican-American, searching for roots is well portrayed in the characters of the play by J. Humberto Robles, *Los Desarraigados* (The Rootless Ones).

This same concern for dignity and respect is found in Corky Gonzalez' "Crusade for Justice" and in the poetry of Alberto Alurista:

> Mis ojos hinchados
>   flooded with lagrimas
> de bronce
> melting on the cheek bones
> of my concern
>   razgos indigenos
> the scars of history on my face
>   and the veins of my body
> that aches
>   vomito sangre
> y lloro libertad
>   I do not ask for freedom
> I am freedom.

And this freedom means education. This freedom means that you and I must become bold, skilled, tough fighters for the educational opportunities that our society says—in abstract, at least—are ours. This means that we must be the advocates, the demanders of a society that honors—not rejects—bilingual, bicultural citizens. We have a great struggle ahead of us—for the basic battleground is the attitude of the dominant Anglo society. A society that equates Anglo-American origin and Anglo-American ways with virtue, with goodness. Other cultures are not merely different: they are inferior. We might have an official language in the United States, but certainly not an official culture. And in the Southwest, according to the much maligned Treaty of Guadalupe Hidalgo, we do have two official languages—Spanish and English.

The time has come for all of us to squarely face the challenge we have avoided or skirted too long. The real problem in our society today—and therefore the real problem in education is not the Negro problem nor the Mexican-American problem nor the Puerto Rican problem—it is the Anglo point-of-view problem. This point of view determines what happens in the school—what emphasis will be given or denied racial, cultural and language values. It is this point of view that through educational activities, social relations in the school, through the subtle, but devastating actions of education personnel, tells youngsters that they are not beautiful because they are different. This is the process that systematically makes it clear that this different youngster is unworthy and unwanted—and so are his parents.

The basic question which you and I must raise again and again—until the issue is resolved is: Is only a monolingual, monocultural society acceptable in America? The answers to this question are streaking across the entire fabric of our society right now. It is very obvious that the melting-pot ideology that we speak of so proudly has not produced a moral climate in which all citizens are accepted on the basis of individual worth. The conflict between youth and the society we have provided for them clearly illustrates the failure of our society—and especially the failure of our schools—to reflect the needs of today's youth. And this failure can be traced directly to the prevailing point of view that to be American is to erase all cultural identity through an education "brainwash." No institutionalized process can make us Anglo. It is imperative that we get this point across loud and clear so the United States will recognize this and we'll begin to fulfill the destiny of a country whose strength lies in its human diversity.

Many of you are here today to explore educational directions and hopefully determine some educational goals. I urge that you exhaust every avenue to secure the maximum education possible. Every *Chicano* is needed. We must become experts in the guerrilla warfare of attitude and behavior change. We must become experts in the psychology and sociology of human relations. We must become bicultural catalysts for a revolution in dominant cultural complacency. We must become experts in the politics of human rights and equal educational opportunities. I can't think of a tougher, but more rewarding role. And your preparation and training for these tasks must begin with your presence and participation in the educational opportunities available right now.

To those of you who have the responsibility of bringing education to our impatient, demanding young people, let me make a couple of observations. You must immediately examine, reexamine and reexamine again your philosophical and practicing basis on which your real and equal educational opportunities are based. And such examinations must be done with full participation of your students. To do less than this, or to delay doing this, will result in only one course—violence and revolution.

Dr. Eugene Smoley, a high school principal in Montgomery County, Maryland, comments on student militancy:

The activists represent a real challenge educationally by questioning the foundations of the society. They're looking for ways to be helpful, pushing for a way for their actions to have some influence, pressing for more meaningful lives. The movement is a very positive thing, because it can only be compared with the apathy of an earlier time.

The United States Office of Education, at the request of Secretary Finch, has set up some task forces to examine some of the critical issues of education. I have been serving on the group dealing with student unrest. Last week I took a whirlwind tour of several cities in the West and Southwest. I spent time talking to college students, teachers, and community people. Whether the responses I received are right or wrong they represent the beliefs and feelings of people. It is interesting to note in identifying the major causes of student unrest as seen by the students, that all of us must accept some part of the blame. Here are the major causes:

1. Failure to accept brown and black community in the educational community.

2. Students see the university as a reject system that is not willing or able to provide educational opportunities for the brown and the black.

3. Special Federal and state programs designed for the high risk students are not functional and cause conflict.

4. Teachers and students are not allowed to participate in determining their own future.
5. The news media have developed an inaccurate picture of student-university conflicts which has escalated the conflict.

It is interesting to note what the students then propose as their role in reducing or preventing conflict and confrontation.

1. Confrontation should only be used when all other alternatives are exhausted.
2. Students should become aware of the lines of authority in order to more adequately present their concerns to the right authority.
3. Students should learn how authority works in order to deal with it adequately.
4. Students should learn how to use the courts as a process of law and order.
5. Students should learn how to use the media to reflect their concerns.

Since the evaluation of the findings is not completed, I wish to refrain from any specific observations on the preliminary information collected. I do feel, however, that there is a wide area for exploration by the university, the student, and the community that holds hope for a relatively peaceful solution to the present educational crisis. I urge that all groups involved take time and effort to find those areas where common agreement can be reached.

The institutions of higher education must meet the challenge. They will have to reassess their very existence: Is their very existence to maintain power? Or is it to meet the demands of the changing times? Institutions of higher learning cannot perpetuate the outmoded methods of the past. They will have to align themselves with the present and with the future.

To date, colleges and universities have made little or no effort to reach the minorities. More effort should be made in disseminating information to the various high schools regarding their programs. The institutions of higher learning must play an active and aggressive role to encourage the Mexican-American to attend their schools, and help must be provided to assure the youth success to compensate for present and past failures of the public school system.

All institutions of higher learning must play a more active and aggressive role in seeking out, assisting in college decisions, and financially supporting the Mexican-American student. It is only through such vigorous movements that the entrance of the Mexican-American will bring to our country the strong fabric of cultural cognizance and thereby enrich our entire society. The *Chicano* is coming out of Tortilla Flats—*now*—you here today represent that movement. Our educational system better be ready—it must do for all of us what it says it is doing for some. *Viva la Causa, Viva la Raza. Gracias.*

SEPARATISM OR INTEGRATION: WHICH WAY FOR AMERICA? [3]

In early 1968, a paper bearing the prophetically disturbing title "Farewell to Integration" appeared in *The Center Magazine*. The author was W. H. Ferry, vice president of the Center for the Study of Democratic Institutions. Admitting that his proposition was sad and that it tended to smash the liberal dream, he nonetheless declared that "racial integration in the United States is impossible," at least in the foreseeable future. He closed his essay—which he labeled "a morose tale"—with a clear warning: We must learn how to manage a separated society "without the sacrifice of freedom and justice for any man. Since we cannot have integration, we must have something."

The philosophy of separatism is strong, claiming support not only from black power advocates but, perhaps reluctantly, from many white liberals. It is an awesome issue, and its resolution will require the keenest insights and most acute reasonings we can muster.

Much has been said and written on the subject during the past year. But the dialogue reprinted below deserves the widest possible reading. It is a clear amalgam of the immense wisdom, experience, and authority of two distinguished leaders in the civil rights movement. Professor Robert S. Browne is an assistant professor of economics at Fairleigh Dickinson University in Teaneck, New Jersey. An executive of the Black Power Conference, he is well known for his logically forthright analyses, through both speech and writing, of the racial dilemmas in America. Bayard Rustin is presently the executive director of the A. Philip Randolph Institute in New York. Long associated with civil rights activities, including the Montgomery, Alabama, bus boycott and the march on Washington, Mr. Rustin is singularly skilled in dealing with groups holding widely different points of view. Among his many other talents is a high competence in extemporaneous speaking.

The dialogue between Mr. Browne and Mr. Rustin took place at a plenary session of the National Jewish Community Relations

[3] Speeches delivered at the National Jewish Community Relations Advisory Council Plenary Session of June 30-July 3, 1968, in New York City. Texts furnished by Mr. Rustin. Reprinted by permission of Professor Browne and Mr. Rustin.

Advisory Council, meeting in New York, June 30-July 3, 1968. Of this debate, John A. Morsell, assistant executive director of NAACP, said:

> We have here calm, reasoned expositions of two diametrically opposed views as to what should be the course and direction of the Negro American's struggle for equality in the present and in the years ahead. [In short, Mr. Morsell concluded] the cause of open, intelligent and honest debate on a deeply felt and divisive racial issue has been materially advanced by the Browne-Rustin debate.

A Case for Separation

ROBERT S. BROWNE [4]

There is a growing ambivalence in the Negro community which is creating a great deal of confusion both within the black community itself, and within those segments of the white community that are attempting to relate to the blacks. It arises from the question of whether the American Negro is a cultural group, significantly distinct from the majority culture in ways that are ethnically rather than socioeconomically based.

If one believes the answer to this is yes, then one is likely to favor emphasizing the cultural distinctiveness and to be vigorously opposed to any efforts to minimize or to submerge the differences. If, on the other hand, one believes that there are no cultural differences between the blacks and the whites or that the differences are minimal and transitory, then one is likely to resist the placing of great emphasis on the differences and to favor accentuating the similarities.

These two currents in the black community are symbolized, and perhaps oversimplified, by the factional labels of separatists and integrationists.

The separatist would argue that the Negro's foremost grievance is not solvable by giving him access to more gadgets, although this is certainly a part of the solution, but that his greatest thirst is in the realm of the spirit—that he must

[4] For biographical note, see Appendix.

be provided an opportunity to reclaim his own group individuality and to have that individuality recognized as having equal validity with the other major cultural groups of the world.

The integrationist would argue that what the Negro wants, principally, is exactly what the whites want—that is, that the Negro wants "in" American society, and that operationally this means providing the Negro with employment, income, housing, and education comparable to that of the whites. This having been achieved, the other aspects of the Negro's problem of inferiority will disappear.

The origins of this ideological dichotomy are easily identified. The physical characteristics that distinguish blacks from whites are obvious enough; and the long history of slavery, supplemented by the postemancipation pattern of exclusion of the blacks from so many facets of American society, are equally undeniable. Whether observable behavioral differences between the mass of the blacks and the white majority are more properly attributable to this special history of the black man in America or are better viewed as expressions of racial differences in life style is an arguable proposition.

What is not arguable, however, is the fact that at the time of the slave trade the blacks arrived in America with a cultural background and a life style that was quite distinct from that of the whites. Although there was perhaps as much diversity amongst those Africans from widely scattered portions of the continent as there was amongst the European settlers, the differences between the two racial groups was unquestionably far greater, as attested by the different roles which they were to play in the society.

Over this history there seems to be little disagreement. The dispute arises from how one views what happened during the subsequent 350 years.

The integrationist would focus on the transformation of the blacks into imitators of the European civilization. European clothing was imposed on the slaves; eventually their

languages were forgotten; the African homeland receded
ever further into the background. Certainly after 1808, when
the slave trade was officially terminated, thus cutting off the
supply of fresh injections of African culture, the Europeani-
zation of the blacks proceeded apace. With emancipation,
the national Constitution recognized the legal manhood of
the blacks, United States citizenship was unilaterally con-
ferred upon the ex-slave, and the Negro began his arduous
struggle for social, economic, and political acceptance into
the American mainstream.

The separatist, however, takes the position that the cultural transformation of the black man was not complete.
Whereas the integrationist is more or less content to accept
the destruction of the original culture of the African slaves
as a *fait accompli,* irrespective of whether he feels it to have
been morally reprehensible or not, the separatist is likely to
harbor a vague sense of resentment toward the whites for
having perpetrated this cultural genocide and he is concerned to nurture whatever vestiges may have survived the
North American experience and to encourage a renaissance
of these lost characteristics. In effect, he is sensitive to an
identity crisis which presumably does not exist in the mind
of the integrationist.

To many observers, the separatist appears to be romantic
and even reactionary. On the other hand, his viewpoint
strikes an harmonious chord with mankind's most fundamental instinct—the instinct for survival. With so powerful
a stimulus, and with the oppressive tendencies congenitally
present in the larger white society, one almost could have
predicted the emergence of the burgeoning movement toward
black separatism. Millions of black parents have been confronted with the poignant agony of raising black, kinky-
haired children in a society where the standard of beauty is
a milk-white skin and long, straight hair. To convince a
black child that she is beautiful when every channel of value
formation in the society is telling her the opposite is a heart-
rending and well-nigh impossible task. It is a challenge that

confronts all Negroes, irrespective of their social and economic class, but the difficulty of dealing with it is likely to vary directly with the degree to which the family leads an integrated existence. A black child in a predominantly black school may realize that she doesn't look like the pictures in the books, magazines, and TV advertisements, but at least she looks like her schoolmates and neighbors. The black child in a predominantly white school and neighborhood lacks even this basis for identification.

This identity problem is not peculiar to the Negro, of course, nor is it limited to questions of physical appearance. Minorities of all sorts encounter it in one form or another—the immigrant who speaks with an accent; the Jewish child who doesn't celebrate Christmas; the vegetarian who shuns meat. But for the Negro the problem has a special dimension, for in the American ethos a black man is not only different, he is classed as ugly and inferior.

This is not an easy situation to deal with, and the manner in which a Negro chooses to handle it will be both determined by and a determinant of his larger political outlook. He can deal with it as an integrationist, accepting his child as being ugly by prevailing standards and urging him to excel in other ways to prove his worth; or he can deal with it as a black nationalist, telling the child that he is not a freak but rather part of a larger international community of black-skinned, kinky-haired people who have a beauty of their own, a glorious history, and a great future. In short, he can replace shame with pride, inferiority with dignity, by imbuing the child with what is coming to be known as black nationalism. The growing popularity of this latter viewpoint is evidenced by the appearance of natural hair styles among Negro youth and the surge of interest in African and Negro culture and history.

Black power may not be the ideal slogan to describe this new self-image that the black American is developing, for to guilt-ridden whites the slogan conjures up violence, anarchy, and revenge. To frustrated blacks, however, it symbolizes unity and a newly found pride in the blackness with which the Creator endowed us and which we realize must always be our mark of identification. Heretofore this blackness has been a stigma, a curse with which we were born. Black power means that henceforth this curse will be a badge of pride rather than of scorn. It marks the end of an era in which black men devoted themselves to pathetic attempts to be white men and inaugurates an era in which black people will set their own standards of beauty, conduct, and accomplishment.

Is this new black consciousness in irreconcilable conflict with the larger American society?

In a sense, the heart of the American cultural problem always has been the need to harmonize the inherent contradiction between racial (or national) identity and integration into the melting pot which was America. In the century since the Civil War, the society has made little effort to find a means to afford the black minority a sense of racial pride and independence while at the same time accepting it as a full participant in the larger society.

Now that the implications of that failure are becoming apparent, the black community seems to be saying "Forget it! We'll solve our own problems." Integration, which never had a high priority among the black masses, now is being written off by them as not only unattainable but as actually harmful—driving a wedge between those black masses and the so-called Negro elite.

To these developments has been added the momentous realization by many of the "integrated" Negroes that, in the United States, full integration can only mean full assimilation—a loss of racial identity. This sobering prospect has caused many a black integrationist to pause and reflect, even as have his similarly challenged Jewish counterparts.

Thus, within the black community there are two separate challenges to the traditional integration policy which long has constituted the major objective of established Negro leadership. There is the general skepticism that the Negro, even after having transformed himself into a white black-man, will enjoy full acceptance into American society; and there is the longer-range doubt that even should complete integration somehow be achieved, it would prove to be really desirable, for its price may be the total absorption and dis-appearance of the race—a sort of painless genocide.

Understandably, it is the black masses who have most vociferously articulated these dangers of assimilation, for they have watched with alarm as the more fortunate among their ranks have gradually risen to the top only to be prompt-ly "integrated" off into the white community—absorbed into another culture, often with undisguised contempt for all that had previously constituted their racial and cultural heri-tage. Also, it was the black masses who first perceived that integration actually increases the white community's control over the black one by destroying black institutions, and by absorbing black leadership and coinciding its interests with those of the white community.

The international "brain drain" has its counterpart in the black community, which is constantly being denuded of its best trained people and many of its natural leaders. Black institutions of all sorts—colleges, newspapers, banks, even community organizations—are experiencing the loss of their better people to the newly available openings in white estab-lishments, thereby lowering the quality of the Negro organi-zations and in some cases causing their demise or increasing their dependence on whites for survival. Such injurious, if unintended, side effects of integration have been felt in al-most every layer of the black community.

If the foregoing analysis of the integrationist *vs.* separatist conflict exhausted the case, we might conclude that all the problems have been dealt with before, by other immigrant groups in America. (It would be an erroneous conclusion, for while other groups may have encountered similar prob-lems, their solutions do not work for us, alas.) But there re-mains yet another factor which is cooling the Negro's enthusiasm for the integrationist path: he is becoming distrustful of his fellow Americans.

The American culture is one of the youngest in the world. Furthermore, as has been pointed out repeatedly in recent years, it is essentially a culture that approves of violence, indeed enjoys it. Military expenditures absorb roughly half the national budget. Violence predominates on the TV screen and the toys of violence are best-selling items during the annual rites for the much praised but little imitated Prince of Peace. In Vietnam, the zeal with which America has pursued its effort to destroy a poor and illiterate peasantry has astonished civilized people around the globe.

In such an atmosphere the Negro is understandably restive about the fate his white compatriots might have in store for him. The veiled threat by President Johnson at the time of the 1966 riots, suggesting that riots might beget pogroms and pointing out that Negroes are only 10 per cent of the population was not lost on most blacks. It enraged them, but it was a sobering thought. The manner in which Germany herded the Jews into concentration camps and ultimately into ovens was a solemn warning to minority peoples everywhere. The casualness with which America exterminated the Indians and later interned the Japanese suggests that there is no cause for the Negro to feel complacent about his security in the United States. He finds little consolation in the assurance that if it does become necessary to place him in concentration camps it will only be as a means of protecting him from uncontrollable whites. "Protective incarceration" to use governmental jargonese.

The very fact that such alternatives are becoming serious topics of discussion has exposed the Negro's already raw and sensitive psyche to yet another heretofore unfelt vulnerability—the insecurity he suffers as a result of having no homeland which he can honestly feel is his own. Among the major ethnocultural groups in the world he is unique in this respect.

As the Jewish drama during and following World War II painfully demonstrated, a national homeland is a primordial and urgent need for a people, even though its benefits do not always lend themselves to ready measurement. For some, the homeland constitutes a vital place of refuge from the strains of a life led too long within a foreign environment. For others, the need to reside in the homeland is considerably less intense than the need merely for knowing that such a homeland exists. The benefit to the expatriate is psychological, a sense of security in knowing that he belongs to a culturally and politically identifiable community. No doubt this phenomenon largely accounts for the fact that both the West Indian Negro and the Puerto Rican exhibit considerably more self-assurance than does the American Negro, for both of the former groups have ties to an identifiable homeland which honors and preserves their cultural heritage.

It has been marveled that we American Negroes, almost alone among the cultural groups of the world, exhibit no sense of nationhood. Perhaps it is true that we do lack this sense, but there seems to be little doubt that the absence of a homeland exacts a severe if unconscious price from our psyche. Theoretically, our homeland is the U.S.A. We pledge allegiance to the Stars and Stripes and sing the national anthem. But from the age when we first begin to sense that we are somehow different, that we are victimized, these rituals begin to mean less to us than to our white compatriots. For many of us they become form without substance; for others they become a cruel and bitter mockery of our dignity and good sense; for relatively few of us do they retain a significance in any way comparable to their hold on our white brethren.

The recent coming into independence of many African states stimulated some interest among Negroes that independent Africa might become the homeland which they so desperately needed. A few made the journey and experienced a newly found sense of community and racial dignity. For many who went, however, the gratifying racial fraternity which they experienced was insufficient to compensate for the cultural estrangement that accompanied it. They had been away from Africa for too long and the differences in language, food, and custom barred them from experiencing that "at home" sensation they were eagerly seeking. Symbolically, independent Africa could serve them as a homeland: practically, it could not. Their search continues—a search for a place where they can experience the security that comes from being a part of the majority culture, free at last from the inhibiting effects of cultural repression and induced cultural timidity and shame.

If we have been separated from Africa for so long that we are no longer quite at ease there, then we are left with only one place to make our home, and that is in this land to which we were brought in chains. Justice would indicate such a solution in any case, for it is North America, not Africa, into which our toil and effort have been poured. This land is our rightful home and we are well within our rights in demanding an opportunity to enjoy it on the same terms as the other immigrants who have helped to develop it.

Since few whites will deny the justice of this claim, it is paradoxical that we are offered the option of exercising this birthright only on the condition that we abandon our culture, deny our race, and integrate ourselves into the white community. The "accepted" Negro, the "integrated" Negro, are mere euphemisms, hiding a cruel and relentless cultural destruction which is sometimes agonizing to the middle-class Negro but which is becoming intolerable to the black masses. A Negro who refuses to yield his identity and to ape the white models finds he can survive in dignity only by rejecting the entire white society, which ultimately must mean challenging the law and the law-enforcement mechanisms. On the other hand, if he abandons his cultural heritage and succumbs to the lure of integration he risks certain rejection and humiliation along the way, with absolutely no guarantee of ever achieving complete acceptance.

That such unsatisfactory options are leading to almost continuous disruption and dislocation of our society should hardly be cause for surprise.

A formal partitioning of the United States into two totally separate and independent nations, one white and one black, offers one way out of this tragic situation. Many will condemn it as a defeatist solution, but what they see as defeatism may better be described as a frank facing up to the realities of American society. A society is stable only to the extent that there exists a basic core of value judgments that are unthinkingly accepted by the great bulk of its members. Increasingly, Negroes are demonstrating that they do not accept the common core of values that underlies America—whether because they had little to do with drafting it or because they feel it is weighted against their interests.

The alleged disproportionately large number of Negro law violators, of unwed mothers, of illegitimate children, of nonworking adults *may* be indicators that there is no community of values such as has been supposed, although I am not unaware of racial socioeconomic reasons for these statistics also. But whatever the reasons for observed behavioral differences, there clearly is no reason *why* the Negro should not have his own ideas about what the societal organization should be. The Anglo-Saxon system of organizing human relationships certainly has not proved itself to be superior to all other systems and the Negro is likely to be more acutely aware of this fact than are most Americans.

This unprecedented challenging of the conventional wisdom on the racial question is causing considerable consternation within the white community, especially the white liberal community, which has long felt itself to be the sponsor and guardian of the blacks. The situation is further confused because the challenges to the orthodox integrationist views are being projected by persons whose roots are authentically within the black community—whereas the integrationist spokesmen of the past often have been persons whose credentials were partly white-bestowed. This situation is further aggravated by the classical intergenerational problem—with black youth seizing the lead and speaking out for nationalism and separatism whereas their elders look on askance, a development which has at least a partial parallel within the contemporary white community, where youth is increasingly strident in its demands for thoroughgoing revision of our social institutions.

If one were to inquire as to who the principal spokesmen for the new black nationalism or for separatism are, one would discover that the movement is essentially locally based rather than nationally organized. In the San Francisco Bay Area, the Black Panther party is well known as a leader in the tactics of winning recognition for the black community. Their tactic is via a separate political party for black people, a format which I suspect we will hear a great deal more of in the future. The work of the Black Muslims is well known, and perhaps more national in scope than that of any other black nationalist group. Out of Detroit there is the Malcolm X Society, led by attorney Milton Henry, whose members reject their United States citizenship and are claiming five southern states for the creation of a new Black Republic. Another major leader in Detroit is the Rev. Albert Cleage, who is developing a considerable following for his preachings of black dignity and who has also experimented with a black political party, thus far without success.

The black students at white colleges are one highly articulate group seeking for some national organizational form. A growing number of black educators are also groping toward some sort of nationally coordinated body to lend strength to their local efforts for developing educational systems better tailored to the needs of the black child. Under the name of Association of Afro-American Educators, they recently held a national conference in Chicago which was attended by several hundred public school teachers and college and community workers.

This is not to say that every black teacher or parent-teacher group that favors community control of schools is necessarily sympathetic to black separatism. Nevertheless, the general thrust of the move toward decentralized control over public schools, at least in the larger urban areas, derives from an abandoning of the idea of integration in the schools and a decision to bring to the ghetto the best and most suitable education that can be obtained.

Similarly, a growing number of community-based organizations are being formed for the purpose of facilitating the economic development of the ghetto, for replacement of absentee business proprietors and landlords by black entrepreneurs and resident owners. Again, these efforts are not totally separatist in that they operate within the framework of the present national society, but they build on the separatism that already exists in the society rather than attempting to eliminate it. To a black who sees salvation for the black man only in a complete divorce of the two races, these efforts at ghetto improvement appear futile—perhaps even harmful. To others, convinced that coexistence with white America is possible within the national framework if only the white will permit the Negro to develop as he wishes and by his own hand rather than in accordance with a white-conceived and white-administered pattern, such physically and economically upgraded black enclaves will be viewed as desirable steps forward.

Finally, those blacks who still feel that integration is in some sense both acceptable and possible will continue to strive for the color-blind society. When, if ever, these three strands of thought will converge toward a common outlook I cannot predict. In the meanwhile, however, concerned whites wishing to work with the black community should be prepared to encounter many rebuffs. They should keep ever in mind that the black community does not have a homogeneous vision of its own predicament at this crucial juncture.

Toward Integration as a Goal

BAYARD RUSTIN [5]

Dr. Browne dealt with the concept of separation in psychological rather than sociological terms. The proposition that separation may be the best solution of America's racial problems has been recurrent in American Negro history. Let us look at the syndrome that has given rise to it.

Separation, in one form or another, has been proposed and widely discussed among American Negroes in three different periods. Each time, it was put forward in response to an identical combination of economic and social factors that induced despair among Negroes. The syndrome consists of three elements: great expectations, followed by dashed hopes, followed by despair and discussion of separation.

The first serious suggestion that Negroes should separate came in the aftermath of the Civil War. During that war many Negroes had not only been strongly in favor of freedom but had fought for the Union. It was a period of tremendous expectations. Great numbers of Negroes left the farms and followed the Union Army as General Sherman marched across Georgia to the sea; they believed that when he got to the sea they would be not only free but also given land—"forty acres and a mule." However, the compromise of 1876 and the withdrawal of the Union Army from the South dashed those expectations. Instead of forty acres and a mule all they got was a new form of slavery.

Out of the ruins of those hopes emerged Booker T. Washington, saying in essence to Negroes: "There is no hope in your attempting to vote, no hope in attempting to play any part in the political or social processes of the nation. Separate yourself from all that, and give your attention to your innards: that you are men, that you maintain dignity, that you drop your buckets where they are, that you become excellent of character."

[5] For biographical note, see Appendix.

Of course, it did not work. It could not work. Because human beings have stomachs, as well as minds and hearts, and equate dignity, first of all, not with caste, but with class. I preached the dignity of black skin color and wore my hair Afro style long before it became popular; I taught Negro history in the old Benjamin Franklin High School, where I first got my teaching experience, long before it became popular. But in spite of all that it is my conviction that there are three fundamental ways in which a group of people can maintain their dignity: one, by gradual advancement in the economic order; two, by being a participating element of the democratic process; and three, through the sense of dignity that emerges from their struggle. For instance, Negroes never had more dignity than when Martin Luther King won the boycott in Montgomery or at the bridge in Selma.

This is not to say that all the values of self-image and identification are not important and should not be stimulated; but they should be given secondary or tertiary emphasis; for, unless they rest on a sound economic and social base, they are likely only to create more frustration by raising expectation or hopes with no ability truly to follow through.

The second period of frustration and the call for separation came after World War I. During that war, 300,000 Negro troops went to France—not for the reason Mr. Wilson thought he was sending them, but because they felt that if they fought for their country they would be able to return and say: "We have fought and fought well. Now give us at home what we fought for abroad."

Again, this great expectation collapsed in total despair, as a result of postwar developments: Lynchings in the United States reached their height in the early twenties; the Palmer raids did not affect Negroes directly but had such a terrifying effect on civil liberties that no one paid any attention to what was happening to Negroes; the Ku Klux Klan moved its headquarters from Georgia to Indianapolis, the heart of the so-called North; and unemployment among Negroes was higher at that period than it had ever been before. It was at that time, too, the Negroes began their great migration to the North, not from choice but because they were being driven off the land in the South by changed economic conditions.

The war having created great expectations, and the conditions following the war having shattered them, a really great movement for separation ensued—a much more significant movement than the current one. Marcus Garvey organized over two million Negroes, four times the number the NAACP has ever organized, to pay dues to buy ships to return to Africa.

Today, we are experiencing the familiar syndrome again. The Civil Rights Acts of 1964 and 1965 and the Supreme Court decisions all led people seriously to believe that progress was forthcoming, as they believed the day Martin Luther King said, "I have a dream." What made the march on Washington in 1963 great was the fact that it was the culmination of a period of great hope and anticipation.

But what has happened since? The ghettos are fuller than they have ever been, with 500,000 people moving into them each year and only some 40,000 moving out. They are the same old Bedford-Stuyvesant, Harlem, Detroit, and Watts, only they are much bigger, with more rats, more roaches, and more despair. There are more Negro youngsters in segregated schoolrooms than there were in 1954—not all due to segregation or discrimination, perhaps, but a fact. The number of youngsters who have fallen back in their reading, writing, and arithmetic since 1954 has increased, not decreased, and unemployment for Negro young women is up to 35, 40, and 50 per cent in the ghettos. For young men in the ghettos, it is up to 20 per cent, and this is a conservative figure. For family men, the unemployment is twice that of whites. Having built up hopes, and suffered the despair which followed, we are again in a period where separation is being discussed.

I maintain that, in all three periods, the turn to separation has been a frustration reaction to objective political, social, and economic circumstances. I believe that it is fully justified, for it would be the most egregious wishful thinking to suppose that people can be subjected to deep frustration and yet not act in a frustrated manner. But however justified and inevitable the frustration, it is totally unrealistic to divert the attention of young Negroes at this time either to the idea of a separate state in the United States, or to going back to Africa, or to setting up a black capitalism (as Mr. Nixon and CORE are now advocating), or to talk about any other possibility of economic separation, when those Negroes who are well off are the two million Negroes who are integrated into the trade union movement of this country.

This is not to belittle in any way the desirability of fostering a sense of ethnic unity or racial pride among Negroes or relationships to other black people around the world. This is all to the good, but the ability to do this in a healthy rather than a frustrated way will depend upon the economic viability of the Negro community, the degree to which it can participate in the democratic process here rather than separate from it, and the degree to which it accepts methods of struggle that are productive.

I would not want to leave this subject without observing that while social and economic conditions have precipitated thoughts of separation, it would be an oversimplification to attribute the present agitation of that idea exclusively to those causes. A good deal of the talk about separation today reflects a class problem within the Negro community.

I submit that it is not the *lumpen-proletariat,* the Negro working classes, the Negro working poor, who are proclaiming: "We want Negro principals, we want Negro supervisors, we want Negro teachers in our schools." It is the educated Negroes. If you name a leader of that movement, you will put your finger on a man with a master's or a Ph.D. degree. Being blocked from moving up, he becomes not only interested in Negro children, but in getting those teaching jobs, supervisory jobs, and principal jobs for his own economic interest. While this is understandable, it is not true that only teachers who are of the same color can teach pupils effectively. Two teachers had an effect upon me; one was black, and the other was white, and it was the white teacher who had the most profound effect, not because she was white, but because she was who she was.

Negroes have been taught that we are inferior, and many Negroes believe that themselves, and have believed it for a long time. That is to say, sociologically we were made children. What is now evident is that the entire black community is rebelling against that concept in behalf of manhood and dignity. This process of rebellion will have as many ugly things in it as beautiful things. Like young people on the verge of maturity many Negroes now say, "We don't want help; we'll do it ourselves. Roll over, Whitey. If we break our necks, okay."

Also, while rebelling, there is rejection of those who used to be loved most. Every teen-ager has to go through hating mother and father, precisely because he loves them. Now he's got to make it on his own. Thus, Martin Luther King and A. Philip Randolph and Roy Wilkins and Bayard Rustin and all the people who marched in the streets are all finks now. And the liberals, and the Jews who have done most among the liberals, are also told to get the hell out of the way.

The mythology involved here can be very confusing. Jews may want now to tell their children that they lifted themselves in this society by their bootstraps. And when Negroes have made it, they will preach that ridiculous mythology too. That kind of foolishness is only good after the fact. It is not a dynamism by which the struggle can take place.

But to return to separation and nationalism. We must distinguish within this movement that which is unsound from that which is sound, for ultimately no propaganda can work for social change which is not based in absolute psychological truth.

There is an aspect of the present thrust toward black nationalism that I call reverse-ism. This is dangerous. Black people now want to argue that their hair is beautiful. All right. It is truthful and useful. But, to the degree that the nationalist movement takes concepts of reaction and turns them upside down and paints them glorious for no other reason than that they are black, we're in trouble—morally and politically. The Ku Klux Klan used to say: "If you're white, you're right; if you're black, no matter who you are, you're no good." And there are those among us who are now saying the opposite of the Ku Klux Klan: "He's a whitey, he's no good. Those white politicians, they both stink, don't vote for either of them. Go fishing because they're white."

The Ku Klux Klan said: "You know, we can't have black people teaching," and they put up a big fight when the first Negro was hired in a white school in North Carolina. Now, for all kinds of "glorious" reasons, we're turning that old idea upside down and saying: "Well, somehow or other, there's soul involved, and only black teachers can teach black children." But it is not true. Good teachers can teach children. The Ku Klux Klan said: "We don't want you in our community; get out." Now there are blacks saying: "We don't want any whites in our community for business or anything; get out." The Ku Klux Klan said: "We will be violent as a means of impressing our will on the situation." And now, in conference after conference a small number of black people use violence and threats to attempt to obstruct the democratic process.

What is essential and what we must not lose sight of is that true self-respect and a true sense of image are the results of a social process and not merely a psychological state of mind.

It is utterly unrealistic to expect the Negro middle class to behave on the basis alone of color. They will behave, first of all, as middle-class people. The minute Jews got enough money to move off Allen Street, they went to West End Avenue. As soon as the Irish could get out of Hell's Kitchen, they beat it to what is now Harlem. Who thinks the Negro middle classes are going to stay in Harlem? I believe that the fundamental mistake of the nationalist movement is that it does not comprehend that class ultimately is a more driving force than color, and that any effort to build a society for American Negroes that is based on color alone is doomed to failure.

Now, there are several possibilities. One possibility is that we can stay here and continue the struggle; sometimes things will be better, sometimes they will be worse. Another is to separate ourselves into our own state in America. But I reject that because I do not believe that the American government will ever accept it. Thirdly, there is a possibility of going back to Africa, and that is out for me, because I've had enough experience with the Africans to know that they will not accept that.

There is a kind of in-between position—stay here and try to separate, and yet not separate. I tend to believe that both have to go on simultaneously. That is to say there has to be a move on the part of Negroes to develop black institutions and a black image, and all this has to go on while they are going downtown into integrated work situations, while they are trying to get into the suburbs if they can, while they are doing what all other Americans do in their economic and social grasshopping. That is precisely what the Jew has done. He has held on to that which is Jewish, and nobody has made a better effort at integrating out there and making sure that he's out there where the action is. It makes for tensions, but I don't believe there's any other viable reality.

Furthermore, I believe that the most important thing for those of us in the trade union movement, in the religious communities, and in the universities is not to be taken in by methods that appeal to people's viscera but do not in fact solve the problems that stimulated their viscera.

We must fight and work for a social and economic program which will lift America's poor, whereby the Negro who is most grievously poor will be lifted to that position where he will be able to have dignity.

Secondly, we must fight vigorously for Negroes to engage in the political process, since there is only one way to have maximum feasible participation—and that is not by silly little committees deciding what they're going to do with a half million dollars, but by getting out into the real world of politics and making their weight felt. The most important thing that we have to do is to restore a sense of dignity to the Negro people. The most immediate task is for every one of us to get out and work between now and November so that we can create the kind of administration and the kind of Congress which will indeed bring about what the Freedom Budget and the Poor People's Campaign called for.

If that can happen, the intense frustration around the problem of separation will decrease as equal opportunities —economic, political, and social—increase. And that is the choice before us.

THE LONG JOURNEY HOME

A TRIBUTE TO DWIGHT D. EISENHOWER [1]

CHARLOTTE T. REID [2]

Dwight D. Eisenhower died on March 28, 1969, at the age of seventy-eight. Thirty-fourth President of the United States, he lived the singularly full life during both peace and war: Allied leader in World War II, president of Columbia University, Supreme Commander of NATO, President of the United States, and in his last years, adviser to the great and a durable friend of the average man.

Eulogies on President Eisenhower voiced a common note: his personal appeal and claim on the affections of millions of people. *Saturday Review* editor Norman Cousins added another dimension of high consequence. He reflected on Mr. Eisenhower's "two pillars of advice":

> the need to keep military-economic power from dominating the national life and the need for developing initiatives of world law as the best means for providing national and world security. . . .

On April 14, 1969, at the annual meeting in Washington, D.C., of the Republican Women's Conference, Representative Charlotte T. Reid of Illinois delivered a tribute to Mr. Eisenhower which captured, simply and warmly, the essential spirit and substance of the man. Mrs. Reid's remarks touched sensitively upon the last journey of the man from the American heartland who chose to return to his home in Abilene, Kansas. And with his passing, as Tom Wicker of the New York *Times* observed, "a good, serene man is lost and mourned; but he was also the last farm boy, and that is why, as he goes to the Kansas earth, something of all of us must go along."

It was just two weeks ago tonight—as dusk settled over the Capitol—that official Washington said a final farewell to

[1] Speech delivered at the seventeenth annual Republican Women's Conference dinner, Washington, D.C., April 14, 1969. Text furnished by Mrs. Reid, with permission for this reprint.

[2] For biographical note, see Appendix.

perhaps the best-loved American of this century. The slow-paced cortege, with its caisson bearing the simple GI coffin, followed by the riderless horse, symbol of the fallen hero—had come to a halt. The solemn processions of the state funeral had reached Union Station. The last echoes of the cannon and bugles had faded away. Now, Dwight David Eisenhower was going home to Abilene for the last time—home to his chosen resting place in the heartland of America from whence he had come.

For three days, heads of state and ministers—great men and women from every part of the world—had come to mourn with citizens from all walks of life—of all races and religions—at the somber Lincoln catafalque in the hushed vastness of the Capitol rotunda—and to raise their voices in the triumphant words of "Onward Christian Soldiers" and "God of Our Fathers" in the majesty of the Washington Cathedral. And as the funeral train began its long and lonely journey across mountain and plain, river and farm, an entire nation stood at attention in final salute—hat in hand, and for most of us a lump in the throat. Yes—in death just as so often in life, Dwight David Eisenhower had once again touched his people deeply.

Each of us here tonight will always have a special memory of General Eisenhower—and each his own personal tribute to one who so joyously took the journey of life, who took it with vision and foresight, and with all the courage and determination at his command.

His deeds were great and many, and historians will so record them. They will tell of Eisenhower the soldier, whose devotion to his country was the motivation of a lifetime in its service—Eisenhower, the commander of the mightiest expeditionary force ever assembled in the cause of freedom—and Eisenhower, the general, receiving the surrender of the Hitler armies in World War II.

They will tell, also, of Eisenhower the educator, as president of Columbia University—one of the nation's great centers of learning and culture.

They will tell of Eisenhower, the crusader for world peace and international understanding and brotherhood while Supreme Commander of NATO.

And they will tell of Eisenhower, our thirty-fourth President, with his magnetic grin, who brought to the nation a welcome period of peace and order—and a strength of purpose and conviction in America.

Yes—every trust we Americans had in our power to bestow was freely given him. It was bestowed because he reflected in his own life and personality the best traditions of a free people—and our nation's faith and hope. We admired his courage of mind and heart, his strength of character, his idealism, his devotion to his family, his belief in the worth of his fellow man, his simplicity, his understanding warmth, and his candor. Everyone "liked Ike"—for most seemed to see in him and his homely virtues some small reflection of themselves. He was so typical of America that each in his own way could see a bit of himself in the soldier-President.

And even in death, I think that General Dwight D. Eisenhower performed one last service which must not go unheeded. Sad though it has been, this period of mourning —with all its memories of the simple heritage of this man from Abilene who brought such inspiration to so many—of his belief in the creed of "duty, honor, country"—of his devotion to the principles on which this republic was built—of the peace and tranquillity which characterized his years in the White House—all this has reminded millions not only of the achievements of a great fellow American, but of our own achievements as well. It has reminded us of our own priceless heritage and the hard-fought origins of our country.

And as he faded quietly away—as old soldiers are said to do—he left with each of us who kept vigil with him a little of his pride in America, a little of his awareness of God, and a little of his responsibility to mankind.

May the Lord bless his memory—and may the Lord give to each of us the strength and courage to carry on those ideals and goals which he lived in life and which were his legacy in death.

Yes—America and the world liked Ike. There can be no finer tribute!

APPENDIX

BIOGRAPHICAL NOTES

BROWNE, ROBERT S. (1924-   ). Born, Chicago, Illinois; A.B., University of Illinois, 1944; M.B.A., University of Chicago, 1947; advanced study, The London School of Economics, 1952; instructor, Dillard University, 1947-49; industrial field secretary, Chicago Urban League, 1950-53; economist, U.S. foreign economic aid program in Cambodia and Vietnam, 1955-61; consultant, Phelps-Stokes Fund, 1963-69; assistant professor of economics, Fairleigh Dickinson University, 1967-   ; author, *Race Relations in International Affairs*, 1961.

CHISHOLM, SHIRLEY (1924-   ). Born, Brooklyn, New York; B.A., Brooklyn College, 1946; M.A., Columbia University, 1952; Professional Diploma in Supervision and Administration, Columbia University, 1960; member, debating society, Brooklyn College; nursery school teacher and director, 1946-53; director, Hamilton-Madison Child Care Center, New York, 1953-59; educational consultant, Division of Day Care, Bureau of Child Welfare, New York City, 1959-64; member, New York State Legislature, 1965-68; United States House of Representatives (Democrat, New York), 1969-   .

FRANKLIN, JOHN HOPE (1915-   ). Born, Rentiesville, Oklahoma; A.B., Fisk University, 1935; A.M., Harvard University, 1936; Ph.D., 1941; LL.D., Morgan State College, 1960; Virginia State College, 1961; A.M., Cambridge University, 1962; instructor in history, Fisk University, 1936-37; professor of history, St. Augustine's College, Raleigh, 1939-43; professor of history, North Carolina College at Durham, 1943-47; professor of history, Howard University, 1947-56; chairman, department of history, Brooklyn College, 1956-64; professor of American history and now chairman, department of history, University of Chicago, 1964-   ; visiting professor at various universities; Edward Austin fellow, 1937-38; Rosenwald fellow, 1937-39; Guggenheim fellow, 1950-51; Fulbright professor, Australia, 1960; member, American Council of Learned Societies; American Studies Association; Association for the Study of Negro Life and History; member, editorial board, *Journal of*

Negro History; author, *The Militant South,* 1956; *Reconstruction after the Civil War,* 1961; *The Emancipation Proclamation,* 1963; *From Slavery to Freedom: A History of American Negroes,* 3d ed., 1967. (See also *Current Biography: 1963.*)

HARDING, HAROLD F. (1903-). Born, Niagara Falls, New York; A.B., Hamilton College, 1925; A.M., Cornell University, 1929; Ph.D., 1937; L.H.D., Hamilton College, 1962; instructor of public speaking, Iowa State College, 1925-27; assistant in English, Harvard College, 1928; instructor of public speaking, Cornell University, 1928-31; assistant professor, 1931-38; associate professor, 1938-44; professor, 1944-46; Chauncey M. Depew Professor and executive officer, department of speech, George Washington University, 1946; professor of speech, The Ohio State University, 1946-66; Benedict Professor of Speech, University of Texas, El Paso, 1966- ; visiting professor, University of British Columbia, University of Michigan, University of California at Santa Barbara; Artillery and General Staff Corps, United States Army, World War II; Army Reserve; on retirement in 1964, Major General commanding 83rd Infantry Division; Legion of Merit (1944) with Oak Leaf Cluster (1964); editor, *Quarterly Journal of Speech,* 1948-51; advisory editor, *Journal of Creative Behavior;* author, *A Source Book for Creative Thinking,* 1962; contributor to *Studies in Speech and Drama in Honor of Alexander M. Drummond,* 1944; *Literary History of the United States,* 1948; editor, *Eastern Public Speaking Conference: 1940,* 1940; *The Age of Danger,* 1952.

KENNEDY, EDWARD M. (1932-). Born, Brookline, Massachusetts; A.B., Harvard University, 1954; LL.B., University of Virginia, 1959; United States Senate (Democrat, Massachusetts), 1962- ; Senate majority whip, 1969- ; member, Senate Committee on the Judiciary; Committee on Labor and Public Welfare; member, board of trustees, Boston University; Lahey Clinic; author, *Decisions for a Decade,* 1968. (See also *Current Biography: 1963.*)

MANSFIELD, MICHAEL JOSEPH (1903-). Born, New York City; student, Montana School of Mines, 1927-28; A.B., Montana State University, 1933; A.M., 1934; student, University of California, 1936, 1937; United States Navy, 1918-19; United States Army, 1919-20; United States Marines, 1920-22; in mining engineering, 1922-31; professor of history and political science, Montana State University, 1933-42; United States House of Representatives (Democrat, Montana); 1943-52; United States Senate, 1953- ; majority

leader, 1961- ; member, Senate Foreign Relations Committee;
member, various delegations to Asia and Europe, including Southeast Asia Conference, Manila, 1954. (See also *Current Biography:
1952.*)

Moos, MALCOLM C. (1916-). Born, St. Paul, Minnesota; A.B.,
University of Minnesota, 1937; M.A., 1938; Ph.D., University of
California, 1942; research assistant, League of Minnesota Munici-
palities, 1938-39; teaching fellow, University of California, 1939-
41; research assistant, University of Alabama, 1941-42; assistant
professor of political science, University of Wyoming, 1942; assistant professor of political science, Johns Hopkins University, 1942-
46; associate professor, 1946-52; professor, 1952-67; visiting professor of political science, Columbia University, 1963-64; administrative assistant to the President, 1958-60; special assistant, 1960-
61; director, policy and planning, Ford Foundation, 1964-66; president, University of Minnesota, 1967- ; co-author, *A Grammar of
American Politics,* 1949; *State and Local Government,* 1952; *Power
Through Purpose: The Bases of American Foreign Policy,* 1954;
The Republicans: A History of the Party, 1956; *Hats in the Ring,*
1960; and others. (See also *Current Biography: 1968.*)

NIXON, RICHARD M. (1913-). Born, Yorba Linda, California;
A.B., Whittier College, 1934; LL.B., Duke University, 1937; prac-
ticed law, Whittier, California, 1937-41; attorney with Office of
Emergency Management, Washington, D.C., 1942; lieutenant
commander, United States Navy, 1942-46; United States House of
Representatives (Republican, California) , 1947-51; United States
Senate, 1951-53; elected Vice President of the United States, 1952;
reelected, 1956; Republican candidate for President, 1960; resumed
law practice, Los Angeles, 1961; member law firm, Mudge, Stern,
Baldwin & Todd, New York City, 1963-68; elected President of the
United States, 1968; author, *Six Crises,* 1962. (See also *Current
Biography: 1958.*)

REID, CHARLOTTE (THOMPSON) (1913-). Born, Kankakee,
Illinois; student, Illinois College, Jacksonville, 1930-32; student of
voice, Chicago, 1933-40; featured radio singer, 1936-39; member
Aurora (Illinois) Women's Republican Club, 1941- , director,
1942-46; United States House of Representatives (Republican,
Illinois) , 1963- ; member, Committee on Appropriations; Com-
mittee on Public Works; secretary, Illinois Republican delegation,
1963- ; trustee, John F. Kennedy Center for the Performing Arts,
Washington, D.C.; national advisory board, Young Americans for
Freedom, Inc.

RODRIGUEZ, ARMANDO M. (1921-   ). Born, Durango, Mexico; A.B., San Diego State College, California, 1949; A.M., 1951; additional graduate work, University of California at Los Angeles; instructor in physical education, San Diego State College, 1947-49; teacher, Memorial Junior High School, San Diego, 1949-54; guidance consultant, San Diego city schools, 1954-57; visiting teacher, San Diego city schools, 1957-58; vice principal, Gompers Junior High School, San Diego, 1958-65; principal, Wright Brothers Junior-Senior High School, San Diego, 1965; consultant, California State Department of Education, 1965-66; chief, Bureau of Intergroup Relations, California State Department of Education, 1966-67; chief, Mexican-American Affairs Unit, United States Office of Education, 1967-   ; United States Army, 1942-44; member, board of directors, San Diego Urban League; president, Council of Exceptional Children, 1954-55; member, board of directors, National Conference on Christians and Jews, 1962-65; president, San Diego Committee for Human Relations Commission, 1963; member, National Education Association; Phi Delta Kappa; contributor to educational publications.

RUSTIN, BAYARD (1910-   ). Born, West Chester, Pennsylvania; member, debating society, West Chester; student, Wilberforce University, 1930-31, Cheney State Teachers College, 1931-33, the City College of New York, 1933-35; field secretary and race relations secretary, Fellowship of Reconciliation, 1941-53; active in formation of Congress of Racial Equality; field secretary, 1941; special adviser to Dr. Martin Luther King, Jr., 1955-60; "chief architect" of Southern Christian Leadership Conference; organizer, March on Washington for Jobs and Freedom, 1963; helped organize first "freedom ride" into South, 1947; executive secretary, War Resisters League, 1953-55; helped organize bus boycott in Alabama, 1955; executive director, A. Philip Randolph Institute, 1964-   ; member, League for Industrial Democracy; National Association for the Advancement of Colored People; recipient, Man of the Year Award, Pittsburgh Chapter of National Association for the Advancement of Colored People, 1964; Eleanor Roosevelt Award, Trade Union Conference of Pittsburgh, 1965. (See also *Current Biography: 1967*.)

WALD, GEORGE (1906-   ). Born, New York City; B.S., New York University, 1927; M.A., Columbia University, 1928; Ph.D., 1932; many honorary degrees, including D.Sc., Yale University, 1958; New York University, 1965; tutor, biochemical sciences, Harvard University, 1934-35; instructor in biology, 1935-39; faculty instructor, 1939-44; associate professor, 1944-48; professor, 1948-   ;

currently Higgins Professor of Biology; national Sigma Xi lecturer, 1952; Overseas fellow, Churchill College, Cambridge University, 1963-64; recipient Eli Lilly prize of American Chemical Society, 1939; Lasker award of the Public Health Association, 1953; Nobel prize in medicine and physiology, 1967; co-author, *General Education in a Free Society*, 1945; *Twenty-six Afternoons of Biology*, 1962. (See also *Current Biography: 1968*.)

WIESNER, JEROME B. (1915-   ). Born, Detroit, Michigan; student, Michigan State Normal College, Ypsilanti; B.S., University of Michigan, 1937; M.S., 1940; Ph.D., 1950; D.Eng., Brooklyn Polytechnic Institute, 1961; associate director, University of Michigan Broadcasting Service, 1937-40; chief engineer, Library of Congress, 1940-42; staff member, Massachusetts Institute of Technology Radiation Laboratory, 1942-45; staff member, University of California Los Alamos Laboratory, 1945-46; associated with MIT since 1946 as professor of electrical engineering, director of electronics research laboratory, and most recently, provost; special assistant to the President on science and technology, 1961-64; recipient, President's Certificate of Merit, 1948; Alfred P. Sloan Award, 1956, 1957; fellow, Institute of Radio Engineers, American Academy of Arts and Sciences; Sigma Xi; Phi Kappa Phi. (See also *Current Biography: 1961*.)

WRISTON, WALTER B. (1919-   ). Born, Middletown, Connecticut; B.A., Wesleyan University, 1941; M.A., Fletcher School of International Law and Diplomacy, 1942; LL.D., Tufts University; special division officer, Department of State, 1941-42; United States Army, 1942-46; associated with First National City Bank of New York since 1946; president, 1967-   ; director, General Mills; member, Council on Foreign Relations.

CUMULATIVE AUTHOR INDEX

1960-1961—1968-1969

A cumulative author index to the volumes of REPRESENTATIVE AMERICAN SPEECHES for the years 1937-1938 through 1959-1960 appears in the 1959-1960 volume.

Acheson, Dean. 1964-65, 53-61, Ethics in international relations today
Allen, F. E. 1960-61, 100-14, Challenge to the citizen

Ball, G. W. 1963-64, 77-90, The reallocation of world responsibilities; 1965-66, 42-55, The issue in Vietnam
Benezet, L. T. 1966-67, 105-17, Acceleration or direction?
Bennett, J. C. 1961-62, 132-47, Christian ethics and foreign policy; 1965-66, 142-55, The issue of peace; the voice of religion
Blake, E. C. 1960-61, 141-55, A proposal toward the reunion of Christ's Church
Boorstin, D. J. 1967-68, 125-35, Dissent, dissension and the news
Bosley, H. A. 1965-66, 157-69, Is God really dead?
Brooke, E. W. 1965-66, 170-86, Crisis in the two-party system; 1966-67, 23-47, Report on Vietnam and east Asia
Browne, R. S. 1968-69, 144-55, A case for separation

Champion, George. 1965-66, 187-99, The consensus complex vs. the free market
Chisholm, Shirley. 1968-69, 68-72, It is time to reassess our national priorities
Collins, LeRoy. 1960-61, 178-88, Speech to the directors of the National Association of Broadcasters
Commoner, Barry. 1962-63, 68-81, Scientific statesmanship
Cooper, R. C. 1961-62, 148-58, "Let's look at the doughnut"
Crichton, John. 1965-66, 210-20, Consumer protection: what Johanna won't read

Dickey, J. S. 1967-68, 136-40, The betrayal of idealism

Eddy, E. D. Jr. 1960-61, 131-40, Our common denominator—the student; 1965-66, 221-5, Student involvement in educational policy
Eiseley, Loren. 1962-63, 39-55, Man: the lethal factor
Eisenhower, D. D. 1960-61, 55-70, Address at the United Nations
Elder, A. L. 1960-61, 165-77, A chemist looks at the world population explosion

Farber, S. M. 1966-67, 118-28, Why national concern for biomedical communication?
Fischer, J. H. 1962-63, 111-21, Educational problems of segregation and desegregation of public schools
Franklin, J. H. 1968-69, 45-54, Martin Luther King and American traditions
Fulbright, J. W. 1963-64, 91-114, Foreign policy—old myths and new realities; 1964-65, 157-69, Education and public policy; 1965-66, 115-41, The two Americas

Gallagher, B. G. 1960-61, 201-12, A preface to the study of utopias; 1967-68, 169-73, Memorial convocation address
Gallagher, Wes. 1966-67, 148-59, Upon the acceptance of the 1967 William Allen White Foundation award for journalistic merit
Gardner, J. W. 1967-68, 102-10, In behalf of a troubled nation
Gaud, W. S. 1967-68, 179-93, Why foreign aid?
Glenn, J. H. Jr. 1961-62, 202-7, Address before the joint meeting of Congress

Goheen, R. F. 1964-65, 113-19, The library and the chapel stand side by side

Goldwater, Barry. 1960-61, 83-99, National objectives in American foreign policy; 1964-65, 35-44, Campaign speech at Madison Square Garden

Gould, S. B. 1962-63, 122-8, A flavor for our daily bread

Griswold, E. N. 1967-68, 141-60, Dissent—1968 style

Gropius, Walter. 1963-64, 182-90, Creative education: key to good architecture and design

Gruening, Ernest. 1965-66, 22-41, United States policy and actions in Vietnam

Hannah, J. A. 1965-66, 93-105, Civil rights and the public universities

Harding, H. F. 1968-69, 121-8, A matter of doubt and grave concern

Heckscher, August. 1961-62, 124-31, The challenge of ugliness

Hesburgh, T. M. 1962-63, 56-67, Science and man

Horn, F. H. 1962-63, 82-96, The prospect for civilization

Howe, Harold II. 1967-68, 111-24, Changing the pecking order

Jackson, E. M. 1965-66, 200-9, The American theatre and the speech profession

Jackson, H. M. 1961-62, 55-63, The United States in the United Nations: an independent audit

Johnson, L. B. 1963-64, 37-42, Remarks to a joint session of Congress; 1964-65, 9-20, An address to a joint session of Congress; 1964-65, 45-51, An address to the nation; 1965-66, 9-21, Vietnam: the struggle to be free; 1966-67, 11-22, Speech at a joint session of the Tennessee state legislature; 1967-68, 11-20, Speech before the National Legislative Conference; 1967-68, 63-77, Remarks to the nation

Kennan, G. F. 1965-66, 56-65, A statement on Vietnam

Kennedy, E. M. 1967-68, 174-8, A tribute to Senator Robert F. Kennedy; 1968-69, 73-88, China policy for the seventies

Kennedy, Gerald. 1963-64, 71-6, Dedicated to a proposition

Kennedy, J. F. 1960-61, 7-14, The new frontier; 1960-61, 35-9, Inaugural address; 1961-62, 7-18, The Berlin crisis; 1961-62, 41-54, "Let us call a truce to terror"; 1962-63, 7-15, An address to the nation; 1962-63, 145-72, A conversation with the President; 1963-64, 9-19, Toward a strategy of peace; 1963-64, 20-9, A step toward peace

Kennedy, R. F. 1966-67, 138-47, The fruitful tension

Kerr, Clark. 1967-68, 86-101, The urban-grant university

King, M. L. Jr. 1963-64, 43-8, "I have a dream . . ."

Lang, W. C. 1960-61, 71-82, "The bold go toward their time"

Ley, Willy. 1960-61, 115-30, The conquest of space

Lindsay, J. V. 1967-68, 78-85, Reality and rhetoric

Lippmann, Walter. 1961-62, 162-70, The frustration of our time

McCarthy, E. J. 1960-61, 30-4, The nomination of Adlai E. Stevenson

McDonald, D. J. 1960-61, 156-64, A plan for prosperity

McGee, Gale, 1964-65, 73-88, An academic looks at Vietnam

McGovern, George. 1963-64, 132-53, New perspectives on American security; 1966-67, 48-69, The ignorance curtain vs. the open door

McGowan, Carl. 1965-66, 227-30, Eulogy on Adlai E. Stevenson

McNamara, R. S. 1966-67, 160-76, Address before the American Society of Newspaper Editors

Malik, C. H. 1963-64, 115-31, Developing leadership in new countries

Mansfield, Mike. 1967-68, 49-62, Assessment in Vietnam; 1968-69, 98-112, A Pacific perspective

Marbury, W. L. 1965-66, 77-92, Of movers and immobilists

Mays, B. E. 1967-68, 161-8, Eulogy on Dr. Martin Luther King, Jr.

Miller, S. H. 1964-65, 138-44, The gospel of insecurity

Minow, N. N. 1961-62, 64-77, Television and the public interest

Moos, Malcolm. 1968-69, 55-67, Darkness over the ivory tower

Morse, Wayne. 1964-65, 62-72, To what purpose war in Asia?

Nakai, Raymond. 1963-64, 49-57, Inaugural address
Nixon, R. M. 1960-61, 15-29, It is
time to speak up for America;
1968-69, 9-19, The antiballistic
missile system; 113-20, Inaugural
address
Nodel, J. J. 1960-61, 213-23, Freedom's holy light
Norstad, Lauris. 1962-63, 129-35,
France-American Society speech

Park, Rosemary. 1963-64, 173-81, Inaugural address
Paul VI, Pope. 1965-66, 67-76, Address before the United Nations
Percy, C. H. 1965-66, 106-14, A Chi-
cagoan goes south

Read, D. H. C. 1966-67, 129-37, Is
God over thirty? Religion and the
youth revolt
Reid, C. T. 1968-69, 165-8, A tribute
to Dwight D. Eisenhower
Reischauer, E. O. 1966-67, 70-81,
Statement before the Senate For-
eign Relations Committee
Rockefeller, N. A. 1962-63, 17-27,
Jobs and prosperity
Rodriguez, A. M. 1968-69, 129-42,
This is our quest: to fight for the
right
Rusk, Dean. 1961-62, 19-26, The un-
derlying crisis: coercion vs. choice;
1964-65, 89-101, An address before
the American Society of Interna-
tional Law
Rustin, Bayard. 1968-69, 156-63, Toward integration as a goal

Sarnoff, R. W. 1962-63, 136-44, Television's role in the American democracy
Scanlan, Ross. 1961-62, 159-61, Public address as a social force
Scranton, W. W. 1962-63, 173-7, Inaugural address
Seaborg, G. T. 1961-62, 110-23, A
scientific society—the beginnings:
the 29th John Wesley Powell lecture; 1964-65, 129-37, The scientist
as a human being
Sears, P. B. 1961-62, 187-201, Science, life, and landscape
Smith, M. C. 1961-62, 27-40, An address to the United States Senate
Snow, C. P. 1960-61, 41-54, The
moral un-neutrality of science

Snyder, J. I. Jr. 1963-64, 154-71, The
total challenge of automation
Stanton, Frank, 1961-62, 78-94, Benjamin Franklin lecture
Stevenson, A. E. 1962-63, 178-83, Eulogy on Eleanor Roosevelt; 1963-
64, 30-3. A tribute to John F. Kennedy; 1964-65, 103-7, Address at
the memorial service for Sir Win-
ston Churchill

Taylor, W. L. 1964-65, 21-34, Civil
rights and Federal responsibility
Toynbee, A. J. 1961-62, 95-109, The
continuing effect of the American
Revolution
Trueblood, D. E. 1964-65, 108-11,
Herbert Clark Hoover

Udall, M. K. 1967-68, 21-48, The
United States and Vietnam—what
lies ahead?
Untereiner, R. E. 1962-63, 28-37, The
public interest in utility regula-
tion

Wald, George. 1968-69, 33-44, A gen-
eration in search of a future
Warren, Earl, 1962-63, 97-110, Ad-
dress at the Louis Marshall Award
dinner; 1963-64, 33-4, A tribute to
John F. Kennedy
Waterman, A. T. 1960-61, 189-99,
Science in the sixties
Weaver, R. C. 1963-64, 58-70, The
Negro as an American
Webb, J. E. 1967-68, 194-208, From
Runnymede to Ganymede
Wert, R. J. 1964-65, 145-56, The
restless generation and undergrad-
uate education
Whitney, J. H. 1964-65, 120-8, Chal-
lenges and excellences
Wiesner, J. B. 1968-69, 19-31, An
argument against the ABM
Wilkins, Roy. 1963-64, 34-6, A trib-
ute to John F. Kennedy
Wirtz, W. W. 1966-67, 177-87, Ad-
dress at the Catholic University of
America
Wrage, E. J. 1963-64, 191-204, Anti-
dote to anonymity
Wriston, H. M. 1961-62, 171-86, Va-
lidity of the educational process
Wriston, W. B. 1968-69, 89-97, A
long view of the short run

Young, W. M., Jr. 1966-67, 82-104,
The crisis of the cities: the danger
of the ghetto